Home Video

Other Books by Marvin Grosswirth

BEGINNER'S GUIDE TO HOME COMPUTERS
THE HERALDRY BOOK
MECHANIX ILLUSTRATED GUIDE TO PATENT AND
  MARKET YOUR OWN INVENTION
FAT PRIDE
THE ART OF GROWING A BEARD
THE TRUTH ABOUT VASECTOMY (with Louis J. Rosenfeld, M.D.)

Home Video

Marvin Grosswirth

DOLPHIN BOOKS
DOUBLEDAY & COMPANY, INC.
GARDEN CITY, NEW YORK

Library of Congress Cataloging in Publication Data

Grosswirth, Marvin, 1931–
  Home video.

  Bibliography: p. 153.
  1. Video tape recorders and recording—Amateurs'
manuals.
TK9961.G76   621.388′33   AACR2
ISBN: 0-385-17285-0
Library of Congress Catalog Card Number 80–2960

Acknowledgments

Much of the credit for the completion of this book goes to Marilyn S. Grosswirth, whose editorial skills and talents, and whose ability as volunteer researcher never fail to astound me. Friend and colleague Norman Schreiber contributed moral support, encouragement, valuable contacts, and heaps of research material.

Special thanks are due to the many manufacturers and distributors who supplied information and illustrations. By way of acknowledgment, each photo caption bears the name of the supplying company.

Special acknowledgment must go to Michael Friddle, whose skills, intelligence, and expertise—all demonstrated during the tedious process of transcribing the tapes on which early drafts were dictated—contributed significantly to the completion of the manuscript. His enormous ability assumes Olympian proportions in light of the realization that despite his contribution to this book, he will never be able to read it—or enjoy any but the audio portion of any video program.

Quotations at the opening of each chapter are from Shakespeare.

Now let us tune in on the wide open world of Home Video.

Contents

Introduction

I do beseech you, as in way of taste,
To give me now a little benefit,
Out of those many register'd in promise,
Which, you say, live to come in my behalf.

—*Troilus and Cressida,* III, iii

The title of this book, *Home Video,* is deceptively simple. Written not for home electronics wizards, it is a *beginner's* guide, intended primarily for people who have heard about, read about, or seen some of the recent innovations—many of them quite startling—in home video and who would like to know more about it and possibly participate in it.

The prospect of home video offers a wide variety of possibilities, ranging from little more than somewhat greater sophistication in home entertainment to the recording and preserving of personal and family histories. For the more ambitious it may offer an opportunity as a supplementary or even a primary source of income. It seems reasonably safe to assume that such people have little or no background in electronics and technology—and not much interest in either. Therefore, this book contains very little about the details of electronics and technology. Its purpose is to acquaint you with a basic understanding of how things work and, more important, what those things are supposed to do. Essentially, this is a book for consumers who want to "buy it, plug it in, and turn it on."

That's what "home video" means. A number of books have been written on the latest techniques for making professional/commercial video productions. This is not one of them. "Home video" refers to pictures and sounds that you can choose to play on the television set in your home—the relatively new and somewhat revolutionary notion that you can exercise much greater control and selectivity over what you watch.

Why, then, "video"? Why not simply "television"? The answer is that video is more—far more—than television. The Oxford American Dictionary defines video as "television, especially television pictures as distinct from sound." That definition is, if not obsolete, certainly limiting. Within the past year or two, video has grown to encompass a whole new conception of television. Indeed, television can properly be regarded as only one aspect of video.

It all has to do with technology. During the 1970s, technology, especially in the fields of data processing (computers) and communications, raced ahead at a mind-boggling rate. Machines have become smaller, smarter, and cheaper. The promise of the 1980s is for more of the same, possibly at an even faster rate. As a result, all sorts of equipment, from computers to television cameras, once regarded strictly as objects of major capital investment, are now small enough to fit into the average middle-class American home and inexpensive enough to fit the average middle-class American budget. These developments are having a profound effect on an important consumer field known as home entertainment.

Until very recently, home entertainment—at least from a commercial point of view—consisted of audio (radio, tape recorders, and high-fidelity and stereophonic phonographs) and television. (Photography probably also qualifies as a form of home entertainment for those given to regaling their friends and relatives with slide shows and presentations of home movies. But even this aspect of home entertainment is being affected by video breakthroughs, as we shall see later.)

Most people are familiar with the developments in audio: If you did not like what you heard on the radio, you could always turn on the phonograph or tape deck and play whatever kind of music suited your mood or requirements. Eventually audio tape recorders became inexpensive enough for most people to own one, so that you could, in effect, create your own audio program. This same progression is occurring in video. We now have much greater variety—and, consequently, selectivity—of program material. We also have the facility of producing our own program material. It is, I believe, a significant indication of the importance of home video as an entertainment medium and market that *Variety,* the newspaper that is generally regarded as the bible of the entertainment industry, now reports on home video in a separate section in almost every issue. It may be true that there is no business like show business, but a business it is, and from a marketing point of view home video is a veritable gold mine.

In 1979 nearly 10 million new television sets were sold in the United States and it is estimated that 77 million American homes own at least one television set. One electronics industry study predicts that by the end of 1987 some 25 million households—about 25 percent of all homes in the United States—will own home video systems. By the early 1990s more than half of all U.S. households are expected to have such systems. In terms of dollars and cents, manufacturers are making some startling predictions. Magnavox, for example, paints the following picture for the video industry for 1985:

• There will be 7 million videocassette recorders in use in American homes and institutions.

• Consumers will have bought 7 million videodiscs.

• Sales of blank videocassettes will reach 56 million and sales of prerecorded cassettes will reach 10.5 million.

• Two million videodisc players will be sold annually, along with 80 million discs to be played on them.

• The total videocassette-recorder market is expected to reach $1.3 billion; the videodisc market is predicted to crest at $2.9 billion.

Thus, it hardly seems surprising that anyone with a stake in the entertainment industry is either actively involved in the home video market or has ambitious plans to participate in it.

The simple fact that it is now possible to

watch one program while taping another is already changing the viewing habits of a large segment of the population. Because people can now be more selective and choose programs better suited to their tastes, more and more entrepreneurs are attempting to cater to those tastes. One of the results is the recent arrival of a new word in the entertainment-business lexicon: *narrowcasting.*

Narrowcasting can best be defined as programming directed toward a specific audience and is perhaps best exemplified by radio. These days most radio stations cling to a specific format: all classical music, all disco, all country and western, all news, all so-called "beautiful music" (usually the kind heard in banks, supermarkets, and department stores), and so forth. Similarly, with the growth of cable and other forms of pay TV, narrowcasting is becoming more evident in television. The eminent financial and business writer Chris Welles predicts that

> the new narrowcasting will consist of dozens, perhaps hundreds, of sharply focused channels serving the television audience's vastly diverse affinities and tastes. Instead of docilely submitting to mindless mass-taste network schedules, the viewer will become his own programmer and create his own schedule from the abundance of much more civilized, intelligent, and imaginative fare delivered by the new technologies. (*Esquire,* June 1980)

The three major networks, CBS, ABC, and NBC (through its parent company, RCA), have already formed subsidiaries for the purpose of supplying programs for videodiscs, videocassettes, and cable and subscription television. Their interests are directed less toward serving the public's artistic and cultural needs and more toward maintaining and improving their profit picture: An ominous Nielsen report has shown that where pay cable television exists, it is drawing away significant portions of the audience from commercial network TV.

Motion picture exhibitors—the people who own and operate movie theaters—are equally concerned about developments in the home video market. According to *Variety,* some major theater chains are considering investing in pay-TV franchises "in communities where theatre audiences are being siphoned off by home entertainment." No less concerned are the producers of those films which exhibitors exhibit. In 1977 not a single motion picture company was involved in home video. By the middle of 1980, however, nine such companies were actively producing and marketing movie cassettes. Six of them have special video departments. As a result, the marketing of motion pictures in video tape cassettes has grown astronomically (see Chapter 4).

In the true spirit of capitalism, all of this zealous competition for the consumer dollar would seem to accrue to the consumer's benefit. A vigorous, competitive marketplace offers the buyer a varied selection and generally good value. Where there are pleasures, however, there are almost always pitfalls. Again, the very same technology that has given rise to all of these benefits has also given rise to some problems.

For one thing, consumers find that, unlike almost everything else these days, prices on electronic equipment keep going down rather than up. Should you buy a videocassette recorder or videodisc player today when, in all likelihood, six months or a year from now the same manufacturer will come out with a new model that will probably have more features and cost the same as, or less than, you would have to pay now? (It is an interesting commentary on the rapid changes in this area that the Consumer Electronics Group of the Electronic Industries Association holds two Consumer Electronics shows every year—in Las Vegas in January and in Chicago in June. These are among the largest and best attended trade shows in America.)

The second problem presented by developing technology is that of incompatibility. As we shall see, there are two videocassette formats; they are not interchangeable. Similarly, there are three videodisc formats; *they* are not interchangeable. In every instance, the company or companies that develop the technologies believe that theirs is best and are gambling on that belief. They are, of course, hedging their bets by involving other major companies through licensing arrangements and the production of accessories and programs for their systems. The consumer, meanwhile, may be confused and uncertain as to which system to go with.

Unfortunately, there are no easy solutions to these problems. In general, the answer must rest with the consumer, although the dilemma of incompatibility is somewhat less of a real problem than it seems on the surface. Apparently, suppliers of tapes and discs are prepared to offer their wares in all formats. If, for example, you wanted to see such films as *Jaws, The African Queen,* or the original *King Kong,* you could easily purchase or rent them in a cassette to fit your machine. Therefore, incompatibility per se is of little or no importance as long as the unit that is finally selected is one of the major formats.

There are, however, no simple answers when it comes to deciding *when* to buy. It is a virtual certainty that the longer one waits, the less one will have to pay and the more technology one will purchase. Carried to ex-tremes, however, allegiance to that truism could result in never buying anything. Probably the best philosophy to follow is: If you want it and can afford it, buy it. Once having done so, put aside all regrets.

Still another problem—more of a nuisance, really—is the fact that home video, like so many other high-technology fields, has developed a jargon, including a few words borrowed from other fields. From the computer field, for example, have come the terms hardware and software. (Hardware is any piece of equipment; software is anything that consists of a program, such as a videotape or videodisc.) I have attempted to ameliorate that problem a little; you will find a Glossary beginning on page 155.

Perhaps the best way to keep abreast of the new jargon, as well as the new technology, is to become a regular reader of any one of several magazines devoted to home video. These are discussed more fully in the Bibliography beginning on page 153 as are several books for those who want to do something more than "buy it, plug it in, and turn it on." (You will find, throughout this book, repeated exhortations to read those magazines. They are often worth twice their price.)

Author's Note

Prices mentioned in this book are manufacturers' suggested retail prices at the time of writing. Substantial discounts of 20 to 30 percent—sometimes even more—are often available, especially in major urban centers.

The photographs throughout this book are intended to serve as examples of the kinds of products described in the text. The depiction in a photograph, or the mention in the text, of a particular brand or product does not constitute an endorsement of that brand or product by the author or publisher. All pictures shown on TV screens in the photographs are simulated.

Home Video

1

TV Sets

Is it thy will thy image should keep open
My heavy eyelids to the weary night?

—*Sonnets*, LXI

It may seem patronizingly obvious to state that at the heart of every home video system is a television set. Of course, you cannot have a home video system without a TV set in your home. Perhaps less obvious, however, is the fact that TV sets these days come in a wide range of sizes, styles, and capabilities. Manufacturers promise all sorts of glorious and wonderful accomplishments for their products. Many of those promises, if not most, are probably real. Whether one *needs* all that is promised and is therefore prepared to *pay* for all that is promised is something else again. In short, we have come a long way since "Felix the Cat."

Few people today remember that "Felix the Cat" figured significantly in the history of television, but he was just one step in a long process that really owes it origins to radio, from which TV evolved in a series of stages and a number of scientific and technological contributions by many groups and individuals. Nearly a hundred years ago, Paul Gottlieb Nipkow, a German, had invented a mechanical scanning device for the transmission of pictures. In 1922 an American named Philo T. Farnsworth developed, at the tender age of sixteen, a scanning system that functioned electronically. A year later Vladimir K. Zworykin, a Russian-born American, invented the *iconoscope* (a television camera tube) and, a little later, the *kinescope* (a TV picture tube), considered to be probably the most significant contributions to TV as we now know it. By 1929 Zworykin could demonstrate a totally electronic and entirely practical TV system.

In the ensuing years, a number of experi-

A 1950s TV atop an early example of "electronics furniture" (see Chapter 9). GUSDORF CORP.

mental television programs were broadcast in the United States and in Great Britain. In 1936 RCA and its subsidiary, the National Broadcasting Company (NBC), began what could be regarded as the first regular TV broadcasts, or "telecasts." They installed about 150 receivers in homes in the New York City area and NBC began telecasting programs from New York, the first of which was a cartoon featuring Felix the Cat.

The progress of television for home use was brought to an abrupt halt by World War II, but almost as soon as the war ended things picked up again. The 1950s are generally regarded as the decade in which television really made itself known on the American home scene. In 1950 there were six million TV sets in operation in the United States. Ten years later the number increased nearly tenfold. By 1980 approximately 77 million American homes had at least one television set.

To fully understand how those 77 million homes can receive sounds and pictures from distant locations requires at least some background in some of the principles of physics. There are many similarities between the transmission and reception of radio programs and the transmission and reception of TV programs. (In fact, the audio portion of TV programs are handled almost exactly the same way as radio transmission.) If you have no such background and want a careful and detailed explanation of how TV works, any good encyclopedia can help you out. What follows here is a basic and perhaps oversimplified explanation. Keep in mind that we are talking primarily about commercial TV rather than a home video system. While most of the basic principles are the same, there are certain technical variations. For example, the description of the TV camera applies to a studio camera. The kind of portable TV camera that is likely to be part of a home video system, while performing the same basic functions and operating on the same basic principles, will have somewhat different innards.

When the light that is reflected from a subject enters a TV camera, the electronic circuitry in the camera converts that light into electronic signals. Most TV stations broadcast "compatible color signals," signals that show up as color pictures on color sets and as black-and-white pictures on black-and-white sets.

The TV camera performs three basic functions. First, it picks up an image of the scene or the subject that is to be transmitted. Second, it converts that image to video signals. Third, it encodes those signals for transmission. The complexity of the required electronic circuitry is too great to include those circuits in the camera itself. Those circuits are situated elsewhere in the TV studio and are connected to the camera by a cable. Inside the camera, through a system of mirrors, the image is separated into red, blue, and green—the primary colors. Then the light images are converted into video signals. These video signals, along with the audio signals, are then carried by cable to the TV station's transmitter. The transmitter combines the separate video and audio signals into a single TV signal. The TV signal is then sent from the transmitter through a cable to an antenna. The TV signal is an electromagnetic wave which is literally broadcast through the air, travelling at the speed of light.

At the same time, the transmitter "boosts" and amplifies the signal, because such signals are capable of travelling only relatively short distances. Even with amplification, the TV signal can cover a distance of only about 150 miles. Furthermore, they travel in virtually a straight line, so obstacles such as hills, dense forests, and tall buildings create interference; the curvature of the earth essentially eliminates potential viewers who are beyond the so-called "line of sight."

To overcome these problems, other methods of transmission are used. *Coaxial cable* is a system of cables through which TV signals can be transmitted over distances beyond the "line of sight" and into regions otherwise inaccessible because of geophysical or architectural hindrances. *Microwaves* are also used. The microwave tower receives the TV signal and converts it to microwaves, which are also electromagnetic. These waves are then transmitted from tower to tower and finally to a local TV station, where they are reconverted to TV signals and then transmitted locally. *Satellites* are, in effect, relay stations in outer space. An earth station transmits television signals to the satellite, which amplifies those signals and then transmits them to another earth station. This permits the transmission of television signals across many thousands of miles. (Cable and satellite TV are discussed in more detail in Chapter 3.)

The now-familiar roof antenna picks up the TV signal and carries it into the TV set in the home. By setting the tuner to a particular channel, you are, in effect, instructing your set to accept only those signals from a particular station, thus blocking out all the others. The circuitry in the TV set reconverts the television signal into the video and audio components and reconstructs the image picked up by the TV camera.

You have probably seen a typical TV picture tube, so you know that it resembles somewhat a gigantic light bulb, except that its wide bottom is flat. That flat portion is the TV set's screen. In the narrow end of the picture tube, or neck, is an electron gun which shoots a beam of electrons onto the screen. A color TV has three electron guns, one each for the red, blue, and green signals. A black-and-white set has only one electron gun.

A TV "picture" is, in fact, not a picture at all. The picture is assembled by the human optical system and the brain from a series of dots illuminated by the electron beam. Imagine that you have decided to paint a blank wall in stripes of alternating colors. You fill a paint sprayer with white paint, spray a stripe across the top of the wall, leave a space, spray another stripe, leave another space, spray a third stripe, and so on, until you have white stripes and blank spaces from the top of the wall to the bottom. You then take a sprayer filled with black paint and, starting at the top, you fill in the unpainted spaces with black paint. In effect, that is what happens on your TV screen. The electron gun "sprays" the electrons on the screen over every other line and then goes back and fills in the alternate lines. But all of that happens in the space of $\frac{1}{30}$ of a second—too fast for the human eye to see it happening—so that all of the lines blend to give a complete picture. On American standard TV, a complete frame, that is, one completed picture, consists of 525 lines. (Other systems, such as those used in Europe, use standards with different line counts.)

The typical TV screen is coated with hundreds of thousands of minuscule phosphor dots. (A phosphor is a synthetic substance that gives off light.) On color sets these dots are arranged in little pyramids of three, one dot each for red, blue, and green. When the electron beam strikes a phosphor, it glows with its appropriate color. The brightness with which it glows varies according to the strength of the beam at the moment of striking. The strength of the beam is determined by the video signal coming from the TV camera. It is these variations in strength that give the variations of color. Again, a major element of TV reception is the human brain, which blends the colors of the individual dots.

A basic home TV system, therefore, consists of a relatively simple set of components: some sort of antenna to pick up the TV signal; a TV tube on which to see the picture; a speaker through which to hear the sound; a channel selector; a volume control; and the necessary circuitry to make it all work together. In effect, that's what virtually every TV set offers. But our society has become so specialized in its needs and desires, and commerce and industry have become so eager for the consumer dollar, that simplicity has given way to complexity. These days TV sets range from ultraminiature portables to gigantic screen systems suitable for viewing in theaters. TVs are available in systems that include stereo phonographs, radios, tape recorders and players, built-in video recorders, portable units that operate from an automobile, boat, or anywhere else and run on rechargeable batteries, sets with earphones for private listening, and even some that will shut themselves off automatically should you doze off during "The Tonight Show." In general, color has essentially taken over from black and white. While black-and-white sets continue to sell, they seem to be bought mostly for special purposes, such as for outdoor use or as supplementary TV sets.

No doubt emulating the automobile manufacturers, TV manufacturers produce new models every year. The changes are often minimal, consisting of little more that an alteration or refinement in cabinet design or the addition of some new gimmick of questionable necessity. To be sure, some changes represent significant technological innovations or improvements. Chances are that those innovations or improvements which prove to be effective will appear as more or less standard equipment on subsequent models. When it comes to really important changes, color TV manufacturers seem to favor five-year cycles. If, therefore, you have a color television that is less than five years old, is in good working order, and satisfies your viewing needs, there is probably no point in replacing it.

"Satisfying your viewing needs" means, for all practical purposes, that the screen is large enough for comfortable viewing by everyone in the room at the time the set is on. You will note that in considering the purchase of a new TV, the first thing anyone talks about is the size of the screen. Occasionally a manufacturer will advertise screen size in square inches, but generally screen size is given as measurement in inches of the distance from one corner of the screen to another, measured diagonally. Color sets generally range in size from about 4 inches to 25 inches; black-and-white sets range from 5 inches to 22 inches. Some specialized sets, no doubt intended for viewers with excellent eyesight, actually have screens measuring about 2 inches. These measurements, by the way, refer to so-called "direct view" TV sets—units in which the image is produced electronically on a screen that you are looking at—as opposed to so-called "projection" TV, in which the image is taken from the screen and greatly enlarged. We shall discuss projection TV in the next chapter.

All TV sets, whether black and white or color, have controls for tuning (channel selection), brightness, contrast, and volume. Color sets have two additional controls: one for color intensity and one for tint. Color intensity controls the depth or saturation of the colors in the picture. Tint, also called hue, adjusts the actual color itself. The color intensity control determines whether the color you see is normal, grotesquely rich, or pastel. The tint determines whether people's faces are flesh-colored, hypertensive red, or a sickly green.

There is a fairly simple way to tune a color TV set. Turn the color controls to the point where the picture is black and white. Then tune for a good black-and-white picture. Gradually turn up the color control until the desired color intensity is obtained. Next, adjust the tint control until flesh tones appear natural, at which point other colors should be properly balanced. An even simpler method, if you are buying a new set, is to look for one that has *automatic frequency control* (AFC) or *automatic fine tuning* (AFT), which, as their names imply, automatically tune the set to the proper color. AFC, incidentally, is a good example of a point that was made earlier. When it was first introduced, AFC was limited to only the most expensive, top-of-the-line sets. These days it would be difficult to find a color TV without it.

If you plan to purchase a new TV, there are several other factors you should consider:

Picture tube. As later chapters in this book will show, the TV set can be used for more than watching reruns of "I Love Lucy" and "Gilligan's Island." If you are thinking of hooking up a computer to your TV, or of using your TV screen as the main battleground for video games, you will require a screen that provides maximum sharpness and that does not cut off pictures at the edges. Most manufacturers are now supplying a new design of picture tube that is shorter and therefore eliminates these problems. By the time you read this, virtually all new TV sets will probably have the shorter tube. However, some dealers may have old stock which they are prepared to unload at extremely low prices. You may be able to get a bargain if you buy such a set, but you may not be able to enjoy your games or computer to the fullest extent.

VHF and UHF. TV stations broadcast on assigned wavelengths. Each wavelength is a *channel*. Channels 2 through 13 are broadcast at *very high frequency* (VHF); channels 14 through 83 are broadcast at *ultrahigh frequency* (UHF). I have not seen a recently manufactured TV set that does not offer the capability to tune in both UHF and VHF channels. Some models, however, especially among those priced lower, may give somewhat shorter shrift to the convenience of tuning in UHF. Whether that is important depends on the number of UHF channels in your area and whether you plan to take advantage of the temptations and delights offered by satellite TV (see Chapter 3).

Color adjustment. In most new TVs, with the exception of the lowest-priced ones, color adjustment is automatic. Usually one of two systems is in play. *Vertical integral reference,* more familiarly known as VIR, is a system that consists of a special VIR signal transmitted by most TV stations for the express purpose of providing automatic color adjustment. VIR-equipped sets receive this signal and the color is adjusted automatically.

Many models also have a so-called "tracking system" that takes over when the set is tuned to a station that does not transmit VIR signals. This system literally keeps track of the color intensity and electronically makes the necessary adjustments for undesirable shifts or changes

Comb filter. A comb filter is a device that keeps the color signal separate from the brightness signal, resulting in an improvement in resolution, that is, the reproduction of details, by about 25 percent. RCA, Magnavox, Toshiba, Quasar, and Zenith are among the companies now equipping sets with comb filters. Within two or three years most sets will probably have them.

Sound. Although recent technological improvements, including transmission by satellite, have brought about considerable improvement in TV sound, high-fidelity aficionados and experts alike are still criticizing the quality of TV sound. At best it can be described as adequate. In 1979 most TV manufacturers devoted serious attention to improving the quality of the sound coming from their speakers. But, as might be expected, high-quality sound is reflected in the price, and the public has not been enthusiastic about paying as much as an additional fifty dollars for better audio. Undaunted, manufacturers are still supplying new models with significantly improved speakers and high-fidelity amplifiers. Among them are Magnavox, Panasonic, Sanyo, RCA, General Electric, Sylvania, Sony, and a number of models sold under the Sears and Montgomery Ward labels. Sony, for example, introduced a 26-inch console model called Matrix Sound which houses a pair of high-fidelity amplifiers and separate speaker systems that provide a stereophonic effect by cleverly delaying, for a fraction of a second, the sound coming from the left and right speakers. But the price for such quality is not low. At the time of its introduction, it carried a manufacturer's suggested retail price of $1,250.

If you are already the proud possessor of a good high-fidelity system, and if it happens to be situated near your TV set, you may still be able to vastly improve the quality of TV sound. A number of TVs now being sold are equipped with jacks (receptacles at the back of the set into which some other component or system can easily be plugged) that enable the owner to plug a high-fidelity system into the TV set. Almost all manufacturers have at least a few sets in their lines so equipped. It is expected that before long such jacks will be universal. This would appear to be an excellent alternative to paying the extra costs of a TV set with a fancy sound system built in.

Channel selection. More and more TV models are being produced with channel selectors that slide or glide from one channel to another the way the tuner operates on a radio. The more familiar type of TV tuner that clicks from channel to channel is mechanical; it is usually the first thing to need repair or replacement because, owing to constant use, it tends to wear out. The sliding type of tuner is based on an electronic rather than a mechanical system and, as is true of most electronic systems, is far less likely to succumb to simple wear and tear through usage. That is a point worth repeating because it is worth emphasizing: Virtually every system or component that functions by means of electronics rather than mechanics is likely to give much longer and better service if it has been made right to begin with. To be sure, when an electronic system or circuit does break down, repairs or replacement are likely to be more costly. It is an equitable trade-off, however, because the electronic system is less likely to break down. In many instances, repairs on electronics are quicker and easier because they are not repairs at all. Frequently a malfunctioning or nonfunctioning machine can be restored to full service by the simple expedient of removing a small board on which a circuit has been printed and replacing it.

Many new models come equipped with push-button tuning. The tuner consists of a key pad which resembles the control panel of a calculator or a push-button telephone. Its chief advantage is that it provides random access to the desired channel without having to go through the intervening channels. In other words, if your set is tuned to Channel 4 and you want Channel 11, by pushing 11 on the key pad, the set immediately goes to Channel 11 without first stopping at Channels 5, 6, 7, 8, 9, and 10.

The up-down scan tuner is a sequential tuner but an extremely convenient one to use. You simply press a button and the tuner scans the range of channels in sequence. When the desired channel is reached, you release the button and the tuner stops.

Remote control. In an era in which millions of Americans are presenting themselves at the altar of physical fitness, millions of others seem to be dedicating themselves to achieving maximum immobility. With an adequate supply of TV programs, potato chips, six-packs, and an efficiently functioning remote-control device, it is possible to place oneself in a chair before a TV set and remain virtually immobile and, indeed, insensible, except to attend to the exigencies of nature. Remote control

This lightweight hand-held programmable scan remote allows viewers to scan through their favorite channels. GENERAL ELECTRIC.

Wireless remote control allows for easy tuning, picture adjustment, and volume control without leaving one's chair—or the adoring *gaze of one's companion.* SONY CORP. OF AMERICA.

means simply the ability to tune a TV set some distance from the set itself—in other words, changing channels without having to get up. Originally remote controls consisted of a wire strung from the remote-control device to the TV set. Electronic tuners led to the development of wireless remote controls. Early wireless remote-control systems were based on ultrasonics, that is, the tuner responded to sound waves, inaudible to the human ear, that emanated from the remote-control device. Unfortunately, sound waves that were all too audible, such as a ringing telephone or the siren of a passing ambulance or fire truck, wreaked havoc on a TV set by causing the channels to flip willy-nilly. Remote-control systems are now based on infrared frequencies and are much more efficient.

Another temporary obstacle to the efficient operation of remote-control systems was the advent of cable TV. To receive cable TV you need a special converter supplied by the cable company. These converters, by and large, are not compatible with most remote-control systems, but newer remote-control systems can accommodate the additional cable channels. A remote control that does not have cable-channel accessibility can often be fitted with a converter at a cost of about $60. Your local TV or video merchant can probably assist and advise you. Ideally, however, if you are about to purchase a new set with a remote-control capability, you may as well get one that is "cable ready," that is, capable of operating on the cable channels, if cable TV is in your area or you expect it to arrive soon.

The remote-control function adds approximately $100 to the price of a TV set. Ultimately the buyer will have to decide which is stronger: the need for exercise or the need for rest.

Gimmicks and gadgetry. Virtually every manufacturer has models with added gadgetry in its line, the practical applications of which are highly subjective. From among these "extra added attractions," two could be considered fairly important. Some new sets come equipped with a jack for cable TV. This eliminates the need for the separate control box supplied by the cable company and therefore gives the viewer one less control to worry about. All other things being equal, anyone with access to cable TV should seriously consider purchasing a set with such a jack.

The second important consideration also involves jacks. In subsequent chapters we will be discussing a variety of attachments and accessories that fit TV sets. Increasingly, manufacturers are introducing at least two or three models in their new lines with built-in capabilities for accepting many of these attachments and accessories. After you have read this book, if you decide you want to own a TV set that readily accepts some of these products, shop around for one that best answers your immediate family viewing needs and that also has the capability of easily "interfacing" with the new add-on features. (*Interface* is another word that has slid from the world of computers into other technologies. The Oxford American Dictionary defines it as "a place or piece of equipment where interaction occurs between two systems, processes, etc." It is a word to remember. You will be hearing it more and more, not just in technological jargon but in general conversation.)

One of the more interesting gimmicks recently introduced is the Zenith Space Phone. For an additional $40 to $50 one can purchase a Zenith 19-inch or 25-inch TV set with a remote control that includes the Space Phone. In addition to hooking up to the usual attachments, the TV set is plugged into a telephone jack. When the telephone rings, the signal is heard through the TV speaker. At the touch of a button on the remote-control unit, the TV sound is cut and the caller's voice is projected through the TV speaker. A microphone located in the set makes it possible for everyone in the room to join in the conversation. This could prove rather interesting in households where the tendency may be to relate the audio to the video regardless of the actual sources of each.

This unusual system features a 19-inch color TV and two 5-inch black-and-white screens. *The cameras are optional.* SAMPO CORP. OF AMERICA.

For those who enjoy talking back to their TVs and want the additional pleasure of having the TV answer, Toshiba may have the solution. "All the viewer has to do," claims a company press release, "is give a spoken command to turn the TV on or off, choose or change channels, or adjust the volume level. The TV set responds to the command—it says 'Okay' when the command is accepted, and says 'repeat' if the command is rejected." Although the press release explains the step-by-step programming of the TV set, the unit's ability to respond to two different voices with a high recognition rate, and its capacity to recognize thirty different words, it does not explain why a command might be "rejected." Inevitably, the mental image arises of a viewer wanting to see the six o'clock news having an argument with his or her TV set which is rejecting commands because it prefers the rerun of "Star Trek." From a somewhat earth-ier point of view, however, one could see the advantage of a voice-responsive TV set to someone who is physically handicapped or temporarily immobilized, as is the case with many hospital patients.

Another interesting new model is offered by the Sampo Corporation of America. It is a TV set with three screens—a 19-inch color screen and two 5-inch black-and-white screens—all operated by remote control. This company's press release declares that "the new three-screen TV has been designed to meet the demands of the typical American family who is always arguing over which programs to watch." There is no explanation as to how the audio portion of three different programs, all being viewed simultaneously, is to be handled. On a perhaps somewhat more practical level is the use of such a TV for those who may need or want to view a major event as it is covered by several channels, as might be the case with news developments or sporting events. Even more realistic is the fact that two small cameras are available for a relatively easy to install closed-circuit TV system. Thus, while the adults are watching their favorite program on the large color screen, they can keep a videonic eye on the baby's room, which would be visible on one of the small black-and-white screens.

As we shall see in Chapter 6, a microprocessor is essentially a tiny computer engraved on a chip about the size of a human thumbnail. Many TV manufacturers these days are taking advantage of microprocessor technology by using these little marvels to control a number of functions within the TV set. But they are also using this technology to add a variety of gimmicks of questionable usefulness, such as digital clocks that offer a constant display of the time, displays of the day of the week, the channel being viewed, and so forth. If you want them, have them. Only remember that each such nicety adds to the total cost of the TV set and, for the most part, does little if anything to improve or enhance the picture and sound.

BASIC BUYING RULES

There are some general rules that should be

TV sets are available in a wide variety of furniture styles. Each of these sets is essentially the same: 25-inch screen, VIR, and other sophisticated electronics. The cabinet styles, however, are all different. GENERAL ELECTRIC.

applied by anyone purchasing a new TV set. They are also applicable to the purchase of all other equipment mentioned and described in this book.

1. Unless you are privy to some sort of special inside information, chances are that in the long run you will be better off purchasing a well-known, well-advertised brand as opposed to a brand you never heard of which is appealing because of a lower price. That lower price may eventually be supplemented by the need for more frequent repairs, limited service facilities, or early obsolescence. Large companies have heavy investments in their merchandise and need to support those investments by offering reliability, quality, and widely dispersed factory-authorized service facilities.

2. It will probably be necessary to make a decision between design and function; ulti-mately you may have to strike a compromise between the two and settle for a model that fits perfectly with your living room decor but is somewhat lacking in some of the features and conveniences you want. Or, conversely, you may wind up with a set that has everything you could possibly hope for but will look a little out of place. Short of achieving downright grotesqueness, I personally tend to favor function over design. (I have been told that my desk—with its digital clock, battery charger, tape recorder, telephone answering machine, and one or two other objects that emit glowing lights, beeps, and buzzes—resembles the cockpit of a 747. So be it.)

3. The size of the screen is a major consideration. It is often difficult to determine whether a TV screen is the right size when it is in a setting other than the one in which it is going to be used. In the store, turn the set on

Many multifunctional portable TVs are available. This one includes black-and-white television on a 3.7-inch screen, AM and FM radio, *and the recording and playing of stereo tape cassettes.* SONY CORP. OF AMERICA.

and stand at a distance that approximates the farthest distance from which the set is likely to be viewed once it is in your home. Watch it for a couple of minutes and see if the image is large enough for comfortable viewing.

4. While you are doing that, study the picture carefully. The image on the screen should be sharp and free of distortion both in color and outline. Try to tune the set to a channel that is broadcasting credits or some other printed material, because lettering is a good test of sharpness. This will also indicate whether any portion of the image is being lost at the edges of the screen.

5. The sound should be checked out in much the same manner as the picture. Try to set it at the volume level at which you are likely to be listening to it. Then check especially for sound distortion.

6. Always play with the equipment you are planning to purchase. It is important to know that you will be able to operate the basic controls comfortably and conveniently. It is also important to get the "feel" of the product. Unless you are a technician, you are not likely to be able to tell, except superficially, whether the model you are looking at is particularly well built. Still, you can, mostly by intuition, determine how it feels to your touch. If it feels flimsy and delicate, or stiff and clunky, you will probably be uncomfortable with it no matter how well it is made. If sales personnel are reluctant to let you get your hands on the equipment, get yourself out of the store and go elsewhere. ("Hands-on" demonstrations are not always practical. Some discount operations require that you come to their establishment with a brand name and model number already in mind, put down your money, pick up a factory-sealed carton, and leave. If you are tempted to purchase a TV set this way because of the usually substantial discount, you should first do some research in places like department stores, where models are on constant display and where everyone is invited to play around with them.)

7. Be wary of sales personnel who make excuses for such store conditions as the existence of fluorescent lighting, interference from nearby buildings or other electrical appliances, and so forth. Sometimes these excuses are legitimate; often they are not. In any case, they should be checked into, especially if they seem to be affecting only one or two sets.

8. Never hesitate to ask questions. A salesperson who is unable to answer your question should be able to get the answer. If he or she can't or won't, get the answer yourself. Invariably it will be available in the instruction manual, the manufacturer's specification sheet on file in the store, or from someone else in the store. It may come as a shock to you to learn that some salespeople are not above creating on-the-spot fiction, making up answers as the need arises to conform to what they think the potential customer would like to hear. One of the best indicators of whether a salesperson is lying or improvising is your own instinct. If in doubt, ask to see it in writing.

9. If you have just about decided that the model you are looking at is right and the price is acceptable, ask to see the instruction and operating manual that comes with the set. It is perhaps a little unfair to take up a salesperson's time while you carefully read the manual, but at least skim through it enough to make sure that installation is easy and the instructions are clear and understandable.

10. Never, never, *never* purchase a major piece of equipment without first reading the accompanying warranty. The terms of the warranty will be attached to or packed with the product, or they may be displayed next to the item you are buying. Certainly it will be on file with the dealer. At the very least, the warranty must describe the following:

A. The guarantees and services that are covered and those that are excluded.

B. The extent of responsibility that the manufacturer assumes in the event of malfunctions and defects in the product or in case of failure to comply with the terms of the warranty.

  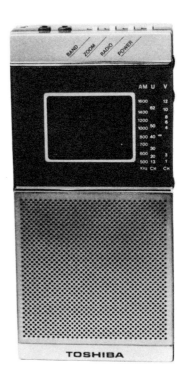

The ultimate in tiny TVs—so far—are these 2-inch-screen units employing a new TV technology: liquid crystal display screens. Dimensions are 6.8 inches long by 3.2 inches wide by 0.7 inches thick. Price? No one knows. These units were shown at the International Consumer Electronics Show in Las Vegas in January 1981, but they are prototypes and the manufacturer has not indicated a production date. The picture quality is far from perfect and the technology needs some work, but by the end of the decade you should be able to carry your TV in your inside pocket or purse. TOSHIBA AMERICA, INC.

C. Those parts, services, and repairs which are free and those which are not.

D. The procedures necessary for having the warranty honored.

The Electronics Industry Association, in one of its pamphlets, offers the following admonition:

BE SURE TO READ AND UNDERSTAND THE TERMS OF THE WARRANTY BEFORE MAKING YOUR PURCHASE!

Antennas. The kind of antenna you will require depends more on your location than on the type of set you use. Virtually all TV sets now come with built-in indoor antennas. These frequently suffice for clear, steady reception. But just as frequently an outdoor antenna will be required. You probably already know from previous experience what kind will best serve you. If you do not, step outside and take a look around. If most of your neighbors have outside antennas, the chances are that you will need one too.

Your antenna should be capable of receiving both UHF and VHF signals. It should also be well constructed and carefully installed, because exposure to the elements will subject the antenna and its connecting wires to deterioration. Once the antenna is installed, it should be checked regularly to make sure that everything is in working order. Look for loose connections, worn or frayed wires, wobbly antenna supports, and so forth.

Separate indoor antennas, that is, those not built into the set itself, are, for all practical purposes, directional. They can usually be moved or turned to achieve the best possible reception from any given channel. This same feature is available on outdoor antennas. It usually involves a motor that rotates the antenna shaft and is controlled by a switch indoors. Such an installation is both difficult and costly.

A variation on this theme has recently been introduced by RCA: a directional antenna called Mini-State. The entire unit, including the rotating motor, is encased in a plastic, weatherproof disclike construction that measures about 21 inches in diameter. The antenna can be aimed by remote control from indoors. There are models that operate on 120-volt AC household current only and those that offer the option of 120-volt AC current or 12-volt DC current for use on trailers, campers, and boats. The unit can be attached to a standard TV antenna mast outdoors or can rest on three legs indoors. The suggested retail price ranges from about $116 to about $140.

As a matter of common safety, outdoor antennas and the lead-in wires should be placed at a good distance from power lines. Measures should be taken to be sure that antennas do not fall onto such power lines, particularly when high winds are doing their mischief. "All outdoor systems should be grounded to provide protection against voltage surges and built-up static charges, including lightning" warns the Electronic Industries Association. "Insist that your installer follow these procedures." This is sound advice that we can only fully support and endorse.

SERVICE CONTRACTS

A service contract is an insurance policy. It is usually issued for a period of one year and it covers those repairs that are either not included in the warranty or that may become necessary when the warranty expires. (It is probably not true that manufacturers design components to break down in 91 days; it only seems that way.) Most dealers can provide you with the name of a company that will offer a service contract for your set. Indeed, many dealers have their own service contract arrangements and may attempt to sell you such a contract without waiting to be asked.

It is important to keep in mind that, as with every other insurance policy, a service contract is a gamble. In essence, you are betting that something will go wrong that would normally cost more to correct than the cost of the service contract. The service contractor is betting that little or nothing will go wrong and the cost of the contract will be mostly profit.

Most new television sets, as well as other consumer electronic equipment and devices, include solid-state circuitry involving transistors, microprocessors, and other electronic elements with relatively few moving parts. Not much can go wrong if your unit arrives in reasonably good condition in the first place. Accidents, of course, do happen and on occasion a lemon is shipped from the factory. Nevertheless, service requirements on most TV sets have diminished considerably.

On the other hand, the more complicated a unit and the more conveniences it provides, the more elements it contains that can go wrong. Furthermore, most consumer products are designed for "normal" use. If your TV set or any other equipment is likely to be operated in areas of extreme temperatures and humidity, or you or the members of your family have already demonstrated a tendency to be accident-prone or simply tend to operate equipment with a heavy hand, perhaps you should consider the service contract. The decision depends, to a considerable degree, on your own feelings of confidence and security.

2

Projection TV

I cannot project mine own cause so well
To make it clear . . .

Antony and Cleopatra, V, ii

Manufacturers and their advertising agencies are inordinately fond of bandying about terms like "giant," "large," "super," and so forth, when describing their TV screens. It is somewhat similar to the way olive growers describe their products: The smallest are classified as large. Such hyperbole would be relatively harmless were it not for the fact that it sometimes causes confusion. For one thing, different people have different notions of what "giant" means. In TV jargon it obviously means a very large screen. But large compared to what? A large screen in a direct-viewing set might be giant compared to some of the 4- or 5-inch models but relatively small when compared to the projection type of TV. It is better, therefore, to set aside such nebulous expressions and turn our attention to specific designations.

In the preceding chapter the television sets described and discussed are the direct-viewing type—the kind that electronically converts a TV signal to a picture on the screen in front of the TV set. In this chapter we will discuss projection-type TV, which, as the term suggests, converts a TV signal to a picture that is then projected onto a large screen.

The principles behind projection TV are not new. As early as the 1940s many TV sets featured small picture tubes that were augmented by some kind of reflecting and/or magnifying system. Projection TV became most popular for special events, such as championship prizefights viewed on closed-circuit television in theaters. It also gained increasing use for commercial and industrial applications.

In 1975 the Advent Corporation intro-

This one-piece projection TV from the company that pioneered in the field is shown next to a person of average height to give an idea of the 60-inch screen size in relation to human proportions. ADVENT CORP.

duced its Model 100A Video Projection TV. This was considered a major turning point in the development of projection TV. The unit cost about $4,000 and was designed for large groups of up to 100 people. It provided a remarkably sharp image on a screen that measured 7 feet diagonally. Shortly thereafter the company introduced smaller, lower-priced models. In succeeding years Advent has continued to offer projection TVs with various refinements and improvements, including inputs for stereo and video equipment.

Advent is regarded as having pioneered in projection TV for the consumer. In the early 1970s it produced a three-tube system developed by an inventive electronics engineer named Henry Kloss. (Mr. Kloss has since gone out on his own and now markets, under his own name, a line of highly regarded projection TV systems.)

By 1979 approximately 40,000 projection TVs were purchased by the public and manufacturers began entering the field with enthusiasm and determination. Many of them are producing systems that are reputed to be of high quality and high technology at relatively low cost. The key word in that sentence is "relatively." In most areas of consumer electronics, prices have tended to come down as technology improves. This has not been the case with projection TVs. Experts predict that the prices for projection TV systems that prevail in the early 1980s—from about $2,500 to around $4,000—are likely to remain in place "for the foreseeable future." There may be some improvements in such areas as channel tuning and perhaps even in picture quality. Nevertheless, a number of systems on the market right now are considered to be of excellent quality and not many significant improvements are expected soon.

FORMATS

There are two formats of projection TVs and two types within those formats. First the formats. The two-piece model consists of a unit that contains the tubes, lenses, and circuitry plus a separate screen. The TV images are projected from the unit onto the screen. The projector must be placed at a certain specified distance from the screen. This distance is not variable and is determined by the size of the screen and the optical system. For example, one 72-inch unit requires a distance of 6 feet between the projector and the screen. Another unit of the same size requires a distance of 9½ feet. Obviously, the first consideration to be made when contemplating the purchase of a two-piece projection TV is whether you have the room for it. On the other hand, two-piece systems tend to be lighter and more portable than the one-piece systems (described in the next paragraph) and there may be circumstances under which that would be regarded as an important or desirable feature. Of course, moving the system about means that every time it is used the projection unit must be carefully and properly aligned with the screen. This screen, by the way, is likely to be made of a material highly susceptible to marks and dirt. Newer units claim to have washable screens; nevertheless, considerable care and gentleness must be exercised in handling and cleaning the screens. If your system is likely to be viewed by children with a propensity for consuming peanut butter and jelly sandwiches while watching cartoons, you may want to think twice about a two-piece projection TV system.

The one-piece projection TV system combines the projector and the screen in a single cabinet. Such systems usually range in screen size from about 45 inches to 72 inches. In one-piece units the TV picture is sent through the lens assembly onto a mirror, from which it is reflected onto a screen. (In some units a rear-screen projection system is employed.) These consoles are, perforce, large and bulky and tend to dominate their environments. They are also rather heavy and not readily susceptible to being moved about. On the other hand, they do take up less space overall than the two-piece system and they do away with problems of misalignment between projector and screen and focusing.

The kind of system you decide to purchase and the size of the screen are variables that only you can determine, since they are dependent upon your own needs. According to Bernard Lee, a motion picture engineer and consultant in optics, projection TV, and home theater design, "In most homes a 4-foot diagonal screen is quite enjoyable. A 5-foot screen is more impressive but it requires a 20-foot room. And if you really want a big crowd, you might consider a 7-foot screen." (*Video Magazine*, January 1980)

THREE TUBES VERSUS ONE

In addition to deciding on format, you will also have to decide whether you want a one-tube or a three-tube system. With the one-tube system the TV image is received on a more or less standard TV set and then, through the use of a single *cathode-ray tube* (CRT) or picture tube and an optical system, it is projected from the surface of the TV screen onto a large and highly reflective screen. The primary advantage of the single-tube system is that it is considerably lower in cost than the three-tube system (described in the next paragraph). The one-tube system has fewer parts and involves lower engineering costs. The main disadvantage of such a system, however, is that its

A deluxe projection TV, this unit features a one-piece, three-tube system; a 50-inch screen; full-function remote control; jacks for video-cassette recorders, videodisc players, and audio equipment; simulated stereo—and a manufacturer's suggested retail price of over $4,000. MITSUBISHI ELECTRIC SALES AMERICA INC.

overall light output is lower than a three-tube system of the same size. A one-tube projection TV is likely to require a lowering of the room lights for adequate viewing. Furthermore, if the scanning or other conditions on the face of the picture tube are something less than perfect, these could be magnified on the screen. Still, given the differences in cost between the two systems, and recognizing that the assessment of picture quality is highly subjective, the single-tube system may prove to be perfectly acceptable. (It is recommended that when considering such systems a prospective buyer inquire as to whether the lens in the system is color-corrected to avoid variations in the transmission of colors to the screen.)

The three-tube system, pioneered by Advent, contains three CRTs—one each for red, blue, and green images. Here, too, the images are projected on a screen with a very high reflectance. The three-tube system avoids certain problems that exist with the one-tube system. The light output is considerably higher and permits nearly normal room lighting. The overall design of the system tends to provide higher picture quality. Understandably, the main disadvantage of a three-tube system is that its cost is considerably higher. Single-tube projection TVs range in price from about $1,000 to over $2,500, whereas three-tube systems start at $2,500 and climb to $5,000 and sometimes more.

This newly developed wide-screen video projection system is capable of showing cinemascope-size pictures in addition to the standard square television screen pictures. Note that the projector is suspended from the ceiling to project a cinema-size picture measuring 2 feet by 5 feet up to 5 feet by 11½ feet, on a slightly concave screen. The projector can also be placed on the floor, but it is probably not suited for use in the average home. SONY CORP. OF AMERICA.

If you decide on the three-tube system, make sure that it includes some method for lining up the three tubes for proper tuning. These methods may consist of a color bar signal, which is an industry standard; a so-called crosshatch signal, consisting of a series of intersecting lines or two single intersecting lines; a series of dots, and so forth. Any method will serve as long as it enables you to perfectly align the color in the picture.

If you have the wherewithal to pay for them, there is no need to sacrifice most of the features and conveniences of standard direct-view TV when purchasing a projection system. Remote control, VIR, audio jacks, and so forth, are all available in projection TV systems. There are also some specialized "output" and "input" features that seem particularly useful when you have an extremely large picture and/or a larger than usual viewing audience. For example, in order to play through your TV, such components as videocassette recorders, videodisc players, video games, computers, and so forth, require that their signals be converted to radio frequencies which the TV set is capable of accepting. But for the large picture a somewhat improved image may be desirable. This can be obtained by a "direct video feed" from, say, a videocassette recorder. Some projection TV units come equipped with an input for such direct feed. This can also be used for "instant home movies" by connecting a video camera directly to the projection system and then allowing your players to cavort.

If you have the need or desire to bring the sound closer to your audience, look for a projection TV model that has an external speaker output. (Remember, however, that it is often possible to connect your own stereo system to a TV.)

Video and audio outputs built into the tuner of a projection TV system will enable you to use the tuner to feed into a portable videocassette recorder that does not have its own built-in tuner. It will also permit the recording of TV sound on video or audio tape, and will enable you to customize somewhat the quality and location of the sound coming out of the system. These various input and output features, however, can be highly seductive; as with most things that are highly seductive, there is a price to pay—in this case, the price, fortunately, is only a monetary one. Consider carefully whether you actually need and will use the features being offered in the immediate or foreseeable future before spending the money they are bound to cost.

SHOPPING FOR A PROJECTION TV SYSTEM

1. Before you venture forth in the marketplace, have a good look at the TV reception you are now enjoying. Whatever problems you may be experiencing, you may be certain that they will be magnified, to the point of grotesqueness, by projection TV. Interference, ghosts, weak or wavering signals—all will assume enormous proportions.

Conversely, if you are now enjoying excellent reception, then that high quality will of course, become even higher with projection TV. If your TV programming now comes via cable, or if you plan to use videocassette tapes or discs (discussed in chapters 4 and 5), a high-quality tape or disc will give you an image that can sometimes be spectacular on a projection TV.

2. In general, observe the rules set forth in Chapter 1. With respect to the warranty, it should be noted that some manufacturers of projection TVs have warranty periods for the tubes that differ from the warranty period for the rest of the unit. It is also important to try to determine whether there is a nearby factory-authorized service agency that is willing to make house calls. Projection TV units, as we mentioned, tend to be fairly heavy and are not conveniently shipped or carried.

3. If you have ever had to sit on the sidelines during a home slide or movie show, then you already know the importance of checking the viewing angle when considering a projection TV. With the set on, stand in front of the screen and then move gradually sideways and note at what point the image drops off significantly. You will have to determine whether the point at which the brightness diminishes is an important factor in the viewing area that you have in mind. (You may want to check for the vertical angle as well.

Recently I was subjected to a demonstration of a one-piece projection TV system that seemed extremely efficient. But the set was turned on after I sat down. During the demonstration I stood up for a moment and was startled to discover that as I did so the image on

Undeterred by the almost futuristic technology involved, manufacturers offer projection TVs (this one is a rear-view 45-inch model) in a wide variety of cabinet styles, including traditional. QUASAR CO.

the screen practically disappeared. If your TV is likely to be viewed by some people sitting on a couch, others sitting on barstools, and yet another group sprawling on the floor, the vertical angle of view can be very important.)

4. Bear in mind that even with the finest three-tube systems, picture brightness will certainly not be the same as that of a direct-view TV of equivalent quality. Try to look at a projection TV under lighting conditions that more or less approximate the conditions in the area where your TV is to be placed. Far too many dealers are not beneath displaying projection TVs in darkened areas well below normal room lighting. The result, of course, is a spectacularly magnificent picture in the showroom and a wishy-washy one in the living room. According to some reports, certain off-brand models will project something approximating an acceptable picture if operated in nearly total darkness. By the same token, however, it is unfair to judge the brightness of a projection TV unit that is displayed in a highly illuminated selling area.

5. If at all possible, try to get a side-by-side demonstration of a projection TV and a direct-view TV. This will enable you to compare the overall picture quality and color of the projection TV system with a direct-view set. While no projection system can duplicate the clarity, brightness, sharpness, or color fidelity of direct-view television, the side-by-side comparison can provide a basis on which to judge the projection system.

6. It is worth repeating that the controls should be checked for ease of operation and accessibility. They can be especially complicated on projection TV units. With single-tube units it is especially important to note whether the TV set at the base of the unit is placed so that its controls are readily accessible.

Anyone even remotely interested in acquiring a projection TV system is likely to pore over catalogues and magazines. Inevitably this will bring one into contact with advertisements for "low cost" projection TV systems ranging in price from $300 to $600. These systems are somewhat different from the kinds that have been described so far. Generally they involve placing a lens assembly in front of the TV set and turning the whole contraption into something resembling a slide projector, with the TV screen acting as the slide. Such systems are generally available in two formats. One consists of a lens assembly that the owner attaches to his or her own TV set. The other is a complete unit that consists of a lens assembly permanently affixed to the front of a TV set supplied by the seller. Both of these systems require a separate screen. It may be possible, with diligent searching and careful purchasing, to obtain a system that provides a reasonably good picture. The quest, however, will be a long, difficult, and frustrating one. At a recent home-entertainment exposition I witnessed a demonstration of one of these systems. The price was extremely moderate. (I will not quote it here in order to avoid identification of the system by its price.) The sales representative demonstrating the unit used a three-sided tent that provided almost total darkness. The image, nevertheless, was noticeably—and, in my opinion, uncomfortably—dark. Most striking, however, was the fact that the picture was extremely fuzzy. I asked the sales representative if the focus could not be sharpened, and he replied, "Of course it can. You can make it very sharp." He made no effort to do so, however. Instead, he offered some excuse about the condition of the TV set as a result of its being transported "from show to show." It seemed to me that while that explanation might be true, the willingness of the company to display such poor quality is an indication of the capabilities of the system and the company offering it. Draw your own conclusions.

3

Pay TV

The law, with all his might to enforce it on,
Will give him cable.

—Othello, I, ii

As America entered the decade of the 1980s, approximately 20 percent of the 77 million homes with TV sets—some 15 million—were hooked up to a cable TV system. And of those approximately one third were paying an additional fee for subscription TV. Apart from the fact that cable TV provides better reception and more variety to the average home viewer, it also offers some interesting insights into the interplay of technology, politics, and avarice.

The cable itself is exactly that—a coaxial cable that consists of a copper wire conductor imbedded in a plastic foam and an outer conductor of aluminum, all of which is enclosed in a protective covering. As the term cable TV suggests, the system involves the transmission of TV signals by means of this cable.

As we discussed in Chapter 1, the transmission of TV signals through the air is limited by distance and is highly subject to interference from physical, architectural, and atmospheric factors. A signal that is transmitted by cable is, of course, completely free of such interference. Let us briefly trace that TV signal from its point of origin to its ultimate destination to see how a cable system works.

By employing a device called a field meter, a cable company determines the location at which TV reception is best for the general area in which it wants to operate. An antenna is erected at that location to receive TV signals in the conventional manner—through the air. Those signals are fed to the *head end,* a building that contains the necessary equip-

Cable-TV subscribers receive a converter like this. The channel selector (tuner) on the converter is used instead of the one on the TV set unless the set is one of the new "cable ready" versions. OAK COMMUNICATIONS, INC.

ment for processing the TV signal. Basically, that equipment consists of a modulator and an amplifier for each channel that is received by the antennas and fed into the head end. Those signals are fine-tuned, amplified, and then fed into the cable. The main distribution cable is known as the *trunk line*. The signals are sent from the trunk line to *feeder lines* and then from the feeder lines to *drop lines*. The drop lines are the lines leading directly to the TV sets. (Most cable systems string their cables along the facilities of utility companies, paying a rental fee for the use of overhead poles or underground conduits.) The converter box that is used by most cable TV systems converts the TV images coming through the cable to an unused channel—usually Channel 3.

In Chapter 1 it was pointed out that TV transmission through the air is essentially a "straight line" or "line of sight" proposition. If the point from which transmission originates can be raised to a great height, then that straight line can cover a greater distance. Ob-

viously there are limitations as to just how high a transmission tower can be built. Ideally, if not practically, the top of a transmission tower should reach into the sky itself. In effect, this has been accomplished.

This ideal height is achieved by a satellite in space. These satellites are relatively small packages containing TV transmitters. They are placed in orbit precisely over the equator at a distance of 22,300 miles. The signals are sent to the satellite, which then sends them back to earth, where, even with the "line of sight" principle, vast areas of our planet can be covered.

Scientists have discovered that the speed with which a satellite revolves around a heavenly body depends upon the distance between the two. The farther away the satellite is placed, the slower it turns in relation to the body. The moon, for example, which is more than 200,000 miles away from the earth, requires a month to complete its orbit. On the other hand, certain meteorological satellites placed relatively close to the earth complete their orbits in an hour and a half. Thus, if a satellite could be placed at the precise distance from the earth, it would revolve at exactly the same speed as the earth and would therefore appear to be stationary. These satellites are known as *geostationary*.

When compared to such earthbound communications media as wire lines, transoceanic cables, coaxial cables, and microwaves, satellites are far and away the least expensive communications medium, despite the fact that they require special earth stations to receive the signals and perform some additional conversions. (For example, the TV signals from satellites are similar to FM signals on radio. This imparts an exceptionally high quality to TV pictures, but it also means that special equipment is required to convert these signals so that your home TV can receive them.) Once the signals are received and converted by the earth station, the transmission procedure is the same as that used for any other through-the-air transmission and for cable.

According to a NASA spokesman, at the end of 1980 there were orbiting around the earth two commercial communications satellites owned by American Telephone and Telegraph, three more owned by Western Union, and three owned by RCA. A TV program beamed to, and back down from, one of these satellites can be seen by anyone within a region bounded by the northern climes of South America to the Arctic Circle and from Bermuda in the Atlantic to Hawaii in the Pacific. Furthermore, these communications satellites are being used for a wide variety of telecommunications, including telephone conversations.

Satellites have already proven to be highly efficient and economical, and more technological advances continue to be made. More satellites are being launched and tests are being conducted on an international level to

An artist's rendition of the Satcom communications satellite in orbit. PHOTO COURTESY RCA.

The Americom South Mountain earth station at Somis, California. PHOTO COURTESY RCA.

develop satellites with more powerful transmitters which will require smaller earth station antennas.

Understandably, television networks and cable companies are taking full advantage of satellite technology. As a result, if one had the proper equipment, one could receive over 150 different channels that are being broadcast by means of communications satellites. And here is where the avarice and politicking come in.

Initially, remote communities received television transmissions via cable through a common local antenna from which TV signals were transmitted. This gave rise to the term CATV (*community antenna television*), a term that is still often applied to cable transmission. These early CATV systems were originally cooperatively owned by groups of local television owners or were under the proprietorship of small, private local operators. Today a number of major corporations are involved in regionwide and even countrywide cable operations. CATV is big business and it involves big money.

Before a cable company can operate within

a community, it must obtain permission to do so from the local authorities. Usually that involves some kind of payback arrangement to the community. There are those who claim that it also involves some kind of payoff arrangement to local politicians for special considerations among competing companies. A separate chapter—perhaps even a separate book—could be written on the wheeling and dealing that obtains when cable franchises are at stake. Subscription TV (which will be discussed next) works best with a cable system and is considered one of the waves of the videonic future. As a result, many large companies as well as small-time operators are scrambling for a piece of the action.

One example of just how lucrative a cable franchise can be was recently reported in *Variety*. In September 1980 the city council of Omaha, Nebraska, voted to award the local cable franchise to Cox Cable of Omaha. The company promised to offer local citizens 108 channels, half of which would be devoted to entertainment and half to a wide variety of data and other services, such as banking, shopping, and so forth. *Variety* gives a list of the investments made by local citizens and what the anticipated return on those investments is likely to be. The chairman of the board, investing $30 for 3 percent of the company, expects a return of $1.5 million. The company's vice-president in charge of human resources (current euphemism for personnel) invested $5 for .5 percent and is looking forward to a return of around $242,000. Others, investing between $20 and $40 are expecting comparable returns. (*Variety,* September 10, 1980)

The viewers who elect to avail themselves of cable TV pay a one-time installation charge (often waived when the cable company is conducting a sales campaign), plus a monthly fee. In Omaha, for example, the monthly rate was expected to be $10.95 for all 108 channels. Cable subscribers can also obtain programming on special channels by paying an additional fee. This is known as *subscription television* (STV) and includes such services as Home Box Office (HBO) and Showtime.

In theory, what makes STV work is the transmission of a scrambled signal. As has already been mentioned, the cable company provides each subscriber with a box, consisting primarily of a tuner, that transfers all of the incoming channels to an unused channel in your TV set. But those who pay for STV receive a slightly different box, one that is equipped with a decoder to unscramble the scrambled signal of the STV channel.

As might be expected, so-called "pirates" have been producing and selling illegal decoders. Just how illegal they are, however, is open to question. One STV company brought suit against a supplier of such decoders in California, where the presiding judge ruled that the signal was public, the case was dismissed. The same operator, however, successfully brought suit in Arizona and was granted an injunction against a Phoenix group of STV pirates. For those who prefer not to run afoul of the courts, STV can be had at a relatively moderate cost, depending on the fare being offered and the use to which it is put. In Omaha, for example, HBO will cost about $7 per month (as compared to about $10 in New York City), and if you like the movies being offered on HBO (which, as a subscriber, I maintain is a very big "if"), then it is certainly a bargain when compared to the cost of going out to see a movie.

The programming available through pay TV is so vast that it would require several pages to list all of it. In any case, such a list would probably be obsolete before it is even published because changes and additions are being made at an incredibly rapid rate. What follows is merely an example of some of the things that are available on pay TV. (Not all facilities are available in all areas—yet.) Uncut, first-run motion pictures, including many that would not be considered appropriate for commercial network television, are available from Home Box Office, Home Theatre Network, Star Channel, Fanfare, Showtime, and other entertainment channels, which also broadcast special nightclub acts and sporting events. There are channels that specialize in sports, news, and financial information, and others that feature religious programs. TV stations in New York, San Francisco, Chicago, and Atlanta, which are independent (i.e., not owned or associated with networks), are available nationally through pay TV; during a typical baseball season, these four stations alone broadcast over five hundred professional games. There are three Canadian channels (one in French, two in English) that are available, as well as a Mexico City station that broadcasts, among other things, bullfights.

A recent brouhaha in the industry was created by the announcement that four major Hollywood movie studios—Paramount, MCA-Universal, Columbia, and Twentieth Century-Fox—along with Getty Oil Company, are forming Premiere STV. The news has sent executives of other STV companies to the brink of nervous collapse; not only does such a combination provide the financial clout for heavy competition, but, more important, the four studios are likely to withhold their own first-run movies for several months after they are shown on their own STV network.

And there is more, much more. There are special children's programs, special women's programs, Consumers Union on HBO and Ralph Nader on Showtime. There is—or will be soon—programming directed at particular ethnic groups. The possibilities are endless. Undoubtedly a good deal of junk will be offered, but it will probably fall by the wayside.

As always, the common denominator here is money. Commercial TV is obliged to reach as many people as possible because the advertisers who pay for air time want to reach the maximum number of potential customers. The result is that those who would prefer something a little deeper or perhaps more enlightening than "Mork and Mindy" tend to be relegated to the Public Broadcasting Service (PBS) channel. But STV has no such constraints; the programming has already been paid for by the subscribers. Theoretically, then, an STV channel could be devoted exclusively to ballet and opera if enough people cared about ballet and opera to subscribe. STV is probably one of the most important elements in significantly changing America's television habits, attitudes, and demands. Its sociological and economic implications are enormous.

While you ponder those implications, here is something else to consider: If the pay TV companies and the networks are taking full advantage of satellite technology, why should anyone have to pay for television? Would it not be a relatively simple matter to build one's own earth station and pick up all of the signals beamed from a satellite? That could mean that the home viewer's choice of channels would be limited only by the number of channels his or her set can tune to (in most cases between 80 and 90 when you combine UHF and VHF channels). Why are there not more privately owned earth stations reaping

the harvest of this seemingly fertile field? There are three reasons: space, laws, and costs.

First, let's talk about space. An earth station requires a parabolic antenna, a device that measures approximately 10 to 12 feet in diameter and looks somewhat like a milk bowl for the Jolly Green Giant's cat. (It is, in fact, usually referred to as a dish.) If you install an earth station in your backyard, chances are you will not have room for much else. If you live in an apartment, forget it. (At least one entrepreneur, however, is offering an earth station for use by co-ops and condominiums that can be installed on the roof of a building.) So much for space.

As to legality, a number of arguments have arisen, all centering on whether the material that is being broadcast is private property. On the one hand, questions of copyright ownership and publication rights arise; on the other hand, the programs travel through the air, which is certainly not private. It has also been argued that the satellites themselves, while privately owned, were put into orbit with government involvement and, therefore, taxpayers' money, and should be regarded as the property of everyone.

Ironically, much of the controversy arises from a law that was passed long before manmade satellites existed. Section 605 of the Federal Communications Act of 1934 prohibits unauthorized individuals from intercepting and divulging or publishing the contents of radio communication. The legal eagles are arguing, both pro and con, as to whether privately owned earth stations are legitimate in the context of Section 605.

Of course, there is also the question of who is likely to prosecute whom. At this writing there are approximately one thousand privately owned earth stations. In the meantime, interested parties continue to develop techniques for scrambling satellite signals. It is my own view that within the next few years satellite technology will improve to the point where it will be much cheaper and will there-

Fred Hopengarten, president of Channel One, standing in an antenna measuring 16.4 feet *across.* CHANNEL ONE, INC.

fore become available to everyone. At the same time, commercial broadcasters—networks, cable company operators, and STV operators—will develop inexpensive ways of scrambling satellite signals. Invariably, an inexpensive way of scrambling signals also probably means the development of an inexpensive way of unscrambling them. But that sort of thing is usually done by buffs and hobbyists. The telephone company, for example, does not appear to be showing any significant dent in its annual profit-and-loss statement because of a few mischievous hobbyists who have found ways to make long-distance telephone calls while bypassing the Bell Telephone System's record-keeping computers. The same will probably happen with satellite

TV. Most viewers will be content to pay for their subscription and enjoy the fruits thereof. By 1990 or so, it should all shake into place. If, however, you prefer not to wait that long, you can own your own earth station now.

BUYING OR BUILDING AN EARTH STATION

Until recently the Federal Communications Commission (FCC) held the intriguing position that it was perfectly legal to own an earth station, but whether it was perfectly legal to use it was something else again. Apart from some questions about getting permission from the program suppliers, the FCC also required that every earth station operator obtain a license from the FCC. Late in 1980, however, the licensing requirement was lifted for "receive only" earth stations. So if you have the space, the inclination, and the money, go ahead and install your own earth station. It is okay with the FCC. Whether it is okay with the commercial interests, however, is another matter. It is possible—although highly unlikely—that they will take you to court.

Prior to 1975, when most satellite TV terminals were installed by international consortiums of communications companies and governments, the cost of installing an earth station was well over $750,000. In 1975, however, cable companies began using satellites and managed to get the cost of the terminals down to about $100,000. Within a year the increasing number of cable systems purchas-

ing earth stations brought the price down even further to around $25,000. Today you can buy a satellite reception system, including installation, for about $12,000.

The basic components are the parabolic antenna, a low-noise amplifier (LNA), and a special receiver. These components can be purchased from a number of supply houses, many of whom advertise in the video magazines. If you want to pay less than $12,000, you can probably obtain the components in kit form. This will require some assembly and some ability with a soldering iron.

The parabolic antenna, or "dish," receives the signals from the satellite. The LNA's function is to boost or amplify the signals from the satellite, which are too weak for adequate reception. The special receiver is a device that re-

A variation of the typical "dish" antenna is this "building block" version. This 8-foot unit can be broken down into 4 foot by 4 foot modules and reassembled into a 12-, 16-, or 20-foot antenna. DOWNLINK, INC.

ceives the output from the antenna and the LNA and then converts the satellite FM signals to the TV signals necessary for reception on your living room screen.

Once installed, your earth station will be positioned to receive the signals from only one satellite. In order to pick up signals from any other satellite, it will be necessary to move the antenna. It may be of some interest to know that in a recent Christmas catalogue Neiman-Marcus offered a fully installed earth station whose antenna could be automatically moved. The price was a mere $36,500.

At the other extreme, there are reports of individuals who have shopped around among dealers of "surplus" electronics and have constructed satellite TV systems at costs ranging from $200 to $1,000. If you have the skill and/or the inclination to do such a thing, you probably ought not to be reading this book.

4

Videocassette Recorders

Sith every action that hath gone before,
Whereof we have record . . .

      —Troilus and Cressida, I, iii

Video tape recorders have been around for a long time. Commercial television has been using them to such an extent that except for news and sports events, "live" television programs are virtually extinct. Essentially, a videocassette recorder is a video tape recorder that has been adapted for home use. In that seemingly simple statement, however, resides a tribute to the near-magical capabilities of modern technology and a recognition of the never-ending scramble for the untold dollars consumers are eager to exchange for that technology.

A videocassette recorder (VCR) has considerable versatility. (The entire video field is fraught with acronyms and abbreviations. Almost everyone refers to videocassette recorders as VCRs, and so, henceforth, shall we.) A basic, "no frills" VCR is capable of:

• operating through any ordinary television set.

• recording off-the-air television programs as they are being broadcast; virtually every model is capable of recording one channel while another channel is being viewed on the TV screen.

• recording images from a TV camera for playing back what has been recorded on videotape that has been properly prepared so that the unit can accept it.

There are, as one might expect, wide variations in these basic functions, depending on the complexity and sophistication of the equipment (and, therefore, its price) and on the interests, tastes, and needs of its owner.

(The VCRs discussed in this chapter all use ½-inch tape in the Beta or Video Home Sys-

An up-to-date version of the pioneering Beta-max. This one offers up to five hours of record-ing from four different stations over a two-week period. SONY CONSUMER PRODUCTS CO.

tem (VHS) formats. There are a number of VCRs that use ¾-inch tape. These tend to be considerably more sophisticated and are intended primarily for professional or advanced amateur use. Many have editing facilities available as either part of the unit or as an add-on accessory. Some prerecorded software is sold in the ¾-inch tape format, but nowhere near the quantities available in VHS and Beta cassettes.)

The acknowledged pioneer in home VCRs is the Sony Corporation, which introduced its Betamax in 1975. The original Betamax was capable of recording up to one hour of programming. In an effort to double the recording capacity (not to mention the competition), about a year later, the Victor Company of Japan (JVC) began offering its Video Home System (VHS) which allowed for two-

hour recording but with a different tape format. Matsushita Electric Industrial Company, JVC's parent, recognizing the enormous potential of its VHS VCR, began a major development and marketing program. Undaunted by Matsushita's encroachment, Sony halved the speed of its original Beta system so that it, too, could now offer two-hour cassettes. Ultimately, despite the efforts of other companies to get into the act, the two original formats, Sony's Beta and Matsushita's VHS, emerged supreme and remain so today.

By the late 1970s most electronics manufacturers had joined either the VHS camp or the Beta forces; the major companies now manufacturing VCRs do so under license to either Sony or Matsushita. Among the firms licensed by Sony to produce Beta format VCRs are Zenith, Toshiba, Sears, and Sanyo.

Companies licensed by Matsushita to produce VHS machines include RCA, Quasar, Panasonic, General Electric, Magnavox, Philco, Sylvania, and Curtis Mathes. With VCRs selling at the rate of about a million units a year, it is not surprising that major corporations are anxious to participate in the fun. (We are referring here only to the "hardware," i.e., the VCRs themselves. The cassettes that can be played in VCRs represent a whole other marketing scramble, which will be discussed later in this chapter.) At present, according to a recent report, the VHS and Beta formats have divided the market on a 60–40 basis, respectively. But why two formats? To understand how they emerged, it is necessary to go back briefly to the beginning.

You are probably already familiar with recording sound on tape. The principle here is the conversion of sound signals to electrical pulses. The coating on recording tape is, in effect, a collection of millions of tightly packed microscopic magnets. These magnets are capable of storing electrical charges. The *recording heads* in a tape recorder convert sound to electrical charges, which are stored in the magnets. The *playback heads* perform a similar function, only in reverse: They convert the electrical charges back to sound.

Those particles, which are microscopic bits of metal, are bound to each other and to the tape itself by being combined with certain chemicals under heat and pressure. Major tape manufacturers continue to make improvements in tape quality and in the density of the materials. For example, iron oxide, once the most common coating substance, has been replaced on many tapes by chromium dioxide and even, in some instances, by all-metal surfaces in which no oxide at all is present.

One of the primary aims of tape technology is to increase the "packing," that is, the number of particles within a given area of tape. The more particles, the greater the recording capability. The greater the recording capability, the greater the possibility of producing narrower tapes. Originally video recording tape was 2 inches wide. Improvements in tape technology have made it possible to reduce tape width to ½ inch—which videocassette recorders now use—without significantly sacrificing picture quality. And several companies are presently developing a ¼-inch tape which will result not only in smaller cassettes but in smaller machines, affording greater portability and versatility. (More about that, too, later.)

There is a special problem with regard to the conversion of the visual image of the TV screen to electrical charges. As you may recall from Chapter 1, these charges of "brightness" move at an extremely high speed: In the space of $\frac{1}{30}$ of a second they cover 525 picture lines on the screen. To capture this movement as magnetic charges on a tape would require a tape moving at an ultrahigh speed; otherwise the charges would "crowd" each other on the tape itself. By using a wide magnetic tape, the charges can be stored laterally across the tape; the recording heads can move at a high speed while the tape itself can move at a somewhat slower speed. With a 2-inch tape, for example, the recording heads move at 240 revolutions per second but the tape itself passes through the recorder at 15 inches per second.

Sony adapted these principles by angling the recording heads in such a way as to spread the signals across the surface of the tape. The effect is something like shining a flashlight directly in front of you and seeing a round spot of light. Now, if you hold the same flashlight at an angle to the surface at which it is directed, you will see that the light forms an ellipse that covers a much wider area. By applying this principle across a tape with ever tinier, tightly packed particles, it was possible to use narrower tapes and smaller units.

With advanced technology, the number of recording heads was reduced from four to two, the width of the tape was decreased, and smaller—and consequently cheaper—units could be made. But Sony held its own patents and when Matsushita was interested in pro-

The Evolution of Videotape. Videotape has increased in usage as it became smaller and more compact. At left is the 2-inch reel introduced to professional broadcasters in 1956 and still in use. One-inch tape was developed in 1964. Videotape in cassettes appeared in the early 1970s in the ¾-inch "U" format. In the mid 1970s ½-inch tape made its debut. Now Technicolor has introduced ¼-inch videotape housed in the cassette in the foreground. TECHNICOLOR, INC.

ducing a tape cassette with a two-hour capability, it had to develop its own format—the VHS.

The basic difference between the two systems is the manner in which the tape is loaded inside the cassette. VHS machines use a system called "M-wrap," so named because the configuration of the tape inside the cassette resembles the letter M. Beta units use the so-called "Omega-wrap" because it resembles the Greek letter of the same name. These different configurations require different mechanics and, to some extent, different electronics. For example, the Beta tapes have aluminum strips at either end. These strips are "sensed" by the VCR, which automatically disengages whatever function button is in use at the moment. The VHS tapes, on the other hand, have clear strips at either end. A tiny lamp mounted inside the unit transmits light through the tape onto a sensor, which, as with the Beta system, disengages the function button.

The most important thing to remember, therefore, is that while in principle the two systems are the same, they are totally incompatible. You cannot use a Beta cassette on a VHS unit and vice versa. This need not be a cause for concern. With respect to software—whether blank cassettes or prerecorded ones—I have yet to see anything on the market that is available in one format that is not also available in the other. You need only remember which format you have and make sure that you obtain the proper software for it.

There is another major difference between the two formats: maximum recording time. VHS machines offer three speeds: standard play (SP), which is the fastest; long play (LP); and super long play (SLP), which is the slowest. Beta VCRs offer only two speeds: faster (BII) and slower (BIII). Using the longest tape and the slowest speed, VHS systems can record up to six hours, whereas Beta systems can only record up to five hours. But some observers feel that the Beta gives a better picture. Also, a number of the functions featured on VCRs are not all operable at all speeds. Consumers Union of United States, Inc., in its *Consumer Reports,* claims that "the Beta recorders and tapes offer what we think is a worthwhile compromise: a somewhat shorter *maximum* recording time (although enough time to satisfy most needs), in return for noticeably better picture quality at the slower recording speed and for all conveniences at all speeds." And Roderick Woodcock, a Canadian technical specialist and a writer in the field of electronics, has written: "In my opinion and on the basis of the test to which I have subjected representative samples, the BIII speed represents the best quality 'economy video' coupled with a well-designed and efficient videocassette system." (*Video* Magazine, December 1980) While these are expert opinions, they are opinions nevertheless. For one thing, the whole question of picture quality is open to debate. It varies as much with location, reception, size of screen,

and age and quality of the TV set as it does with what each individual is prepared to demand or settle for. Some critics have found that the VCR provides better audio reproduction. Furthermore, within the two formats there are many variations on the conveniences and functions packed into any given unit; the importance and desirability of these functions are also highly subjective. In the final analysis, then, your own needs, tastes, and budget will be the most important determining factors.

Before you actually purchase a VCR, take your time. Shop around as much as possible. There are over a dozen brands on the market and several models within each brand. Keep in mind that, as with TV sets, manufacturers are constantly redevising and redesigning their models. Sometimes the differences are merely design changes—what the industry aptly calls "cosmetics." That could be important if size, dimensions, weight, compatibility with home decor, and so forth, matter. You should understand exactly what you are paying for before you pay for it. Know exactly what your VCR will and will not do. Most important, when considering the things that it will do, be sure you need or want all of the features that are offered. Each of these features adds something to the final price. On the other hand, if you are willing to pay less with the understanding that you will get less, make sure you are not sacrificing any features that you will soon want.

Among the features that are already available, or will be in the near future, are high portability, the ability to increase playing time by stacking and then automatically changing cassettes, scanning capabilities in both forward and reverse, and high speeds. Some units have already replaced mechanical functions with electronic ones. For example, electronic tuners make it possible to go from one mode of operation to another without having to go through the "stop" function. Some models automatically rewind the tape when it reaches the end. When purchasing a VCR, you could easily spend anywhere between $700 and $1,500. The wide range in price is an indica-

These VCRs, all from the same manufacturer, indicate some of the differences among various models. The unit in center foreground offers thirteen remote-control "special effects" and can be programmed for eight off-the-air tap- *ings over a two-week period. The unit on the right is the same, except that it has only four remote-control functions. The VCR on the left is programmable once up to one day in advance.* QUASAR CO.

tion of the wide range in performance and the variety of appurtenances and gimmicks that are included.

Another tribute to recent technology is the fact that VCRs can now be divided into two general categories (in addition, of course, to the two formats): consoles and portables. The consoles tend to be rather heavy, weighing approximately forty pounds. The portables, on the other hand, are extremely light, weighing about fifteen pounds or even less. For "on location" taping a portable VCR is virtually mandatory. (The TV camera itself receives images, converts them to electronic signals, and sends them out again. It does not store these images as does the film in a motion picture camera. All of this is discussed in Chapter 8.) However, the consoles are capable of much more versatility than are the portables. Again, a trade-off of what you need most may

be necessary. Or, if you have the funds, the space, and the inclination, you could get one of each type.

THE BASIC VCR

If all of this seems confusing, take heart. It is. With all of the variations and gadgetry that manufacturers are dangling at the end of their hooks in order to entice consumer dollars, it is difficult to sort out who has what and who needs which. Here is a list of what all VCRs should have and what many do have.

Controls. The basic controls on a VCR are similar to those of an audio cassette recorder: "on" and "off," "record," "play," "rewind," "fast forward," "eject," and so forth.

Recording. Every VCR will permit the recording of at least one channel while viewing another. Beta format allows a maximum of five hours of recording on a single tape; VHS allows six hours. Most units in both systems offer advanced programming features. This means that the VCR can be set in advance to record during at least one time period from at least one channel.

Remote control. Remote-control devices are available for both formats. But not every function can be remotely controlled all the time. Some functions that can be used during one playing or recording speed may not be usable during another.

Recording speed. Both formats offer variations in recording speed. The advantage to recording at a slower speed is that you get more recorded material on a given quantity of tape. The disadvantage is that the slower the speed, the lower the quality of the recording.

Pause. Most VCRs include a "pause" feature. When the pause control is activated during the viewing of a tape, the scene on the TV screen instantly stops. (In motion picture and television jargon, this is called a freeze-frame.) It is a particularly useful feature should it be

necessary or desirable to interrupt your viewing and then pick up where you left off. If you are recording a program at the same time it is being broadcast, by activating the pause feature, you can eliminate commercials and station breaks from your recording.

Counter. Most VCRs come equipped with a digital counter. If you set the counter to zero at the beginning of the tape, by noting the number on the counter at any given point on the tape you can return to that point at some future time.

Memory. Most VCRs have a memory feature. When the unit is in the playback or record mode, and you reach a point on the tape that you will want to see again, you need only reset the tape counter to zero and turn on the memory switch. After that, when you rewind —provided the memory switch is still on—the tape will stop at the point you previously selected.

Cue/Review. This feature permits you to advance or reverse the tape at a speed much higher than normal while still seeing the pic-

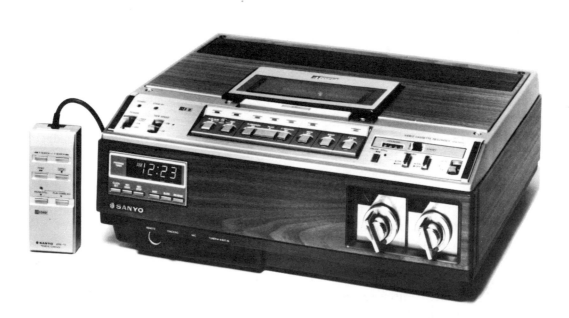

The remote-control unit attached to this VCR duplicates many of the function switches located on the unit itself. SANYO ELECTRIC, INC.

ture. The picture and sound quality are hardly acceptable during cue/review, but the primary advantage of this feature is that it allows you to rapidly find what you are looking for. It also enables you to quickly bypass commercials and station breaks. That could cut the viewing time of a feature-length film, for example, from 2½ to about 1½ hours.

Dew light. This is an indicator that signals the presence of moisture in the VCR. Moisture can cause serious damage to recording tapes and sometimes even to the unit itself.

Slow motion. Many VCRs are capable of slowing up the action in the playback mode. This could prove useful should there be a need to analyze or study any particular action or to achieve some desired special effect.

Frame advance. This is a variation of slow motion. It is similar to a series of freeze-frames, except that the frame changes every few seconds. This could be especially useful for those who want to edit their own tapes. (See Chapter 10.)

Fast motion. Most VHS consoles and a few Betamax models are capable of doubling or tripling the speed with which the action occurs. This, too, can help get you past recorded station breaks and commercials. If you are watching a football game that you think ought to have a little more action, it is a convenient way to get the players to move faster.

Cassette ejection. Some Beta VCRs automatically eject the cassette when the tape comes to an end. This makes it possible to equip the unit with an accessory cassette changer for recording periods when no one is around to replace a fully recorded tape with a blank one. (See Chapter 9.)

Audio dubbing. This feature, which can be found on many VCRs, enables you to record a sound track on a tape so that you can provide your own background music, special sound effects, or narration.

PORTABLE VCRs

The need to pick up a VCR and carry it around is directly connected to the need or desire to produce one's own videocassettes during on-location shooting. There are, of course, other uses. Sales personnel, for example, may readily find offices and shops with TV sets but without much other video equipment. A portable VCR can easily be hooked up to anyone else's TV set as the salesperson makes his rounds. A portable VCR can also be a useful educational tool.

Obviously, the primary advantage of a portable VCR is its portability. Some of them weigh as little as nine or ten pounds and manufacturers are promising even lighter ones. In general, they operate from a variety of power sources, including self-contained rechargeable battery packs, supplementary batteries, and direct current (DC) sources such as boat batteries. Almost all of them can also be used, with a proper adaptor, on ordinary household alternating current (AC). The main disadvantage of the portable units is that their portability is largely achieved by eliminating many of the features of the full-size VCRs. Chief among these is the tuner/timer unit. This is the control on a VCR that tunes to the desired channel and times the length of the recording. Most portable units, however, readily plug into an accessory tuner/timer-AC adaptor combination for the usual recording of off-the-air material and the playing of recorded cassettes. Most portable VCRs use standard Beta or VHS cassettes. The portables range in price from about $600 to $1,000.

Manufacturers have been hard at work for several years to produce a ¼-inch tape for use in even smaller and lighter VCRs. The first to reach the market is the Technicolor Model 212 Video Recorder. The recorder, with battery, weighs about seven pounds and can record for half an hour on ¼-inch tape in a cassette that looks very much like a standard audio cassette. Technicolor's "package," which includes the VCR, a power adaptor, battery, switch box, a cassette tape, a shoulder strap, and an assortment of cables and connectors, lists for $995. Technicolor's camera is an additional $950. There are other accessories as well. No doubt the competition is

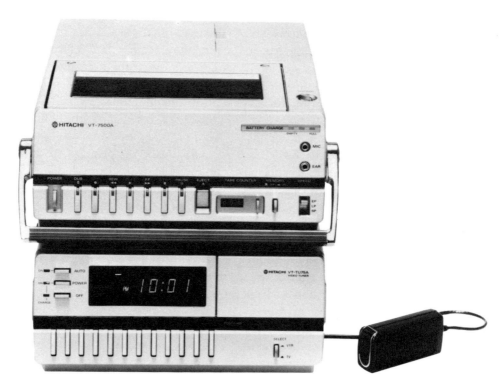

Portable VCRs omit the tuners necessary to tune in TV programs. Accessory tuners can, of course, be purchased. Typically, the VCR sits atop the tuner, as shown here. HITACHI SALES CORP. OF AMERICA.

keeping a careful watch on Technicolor's success with its Model 212 system. Several major manufacturers are hard at work developing their own ¼-inch tape technology. It is expected that these developments will lead to the kind of video system that is likely to appeal to an even broader market than the existing VCRs. If the tape and recording components can be made small enough, it should be possible to produce a video camera that is self-contained, that is, one that contains the storage medium within the camera in the same way that movie cameras do. Sony has already shown its single-unit camera, but it is only a prototype and is not expected to be ready for the market until about 1985. Hitachi has promised to produce its self-contained camera "earlier."

In the meantime, the ¼-inch-tape portables present the problem of incompatibility. You cannot use a ¼-inch tape on equipment designed for ½-inch tape. You can, however, interface such equipment. By buying or renting another VCR, it is a fairly simple matter to transfer material from a ¼-inch tape to a more standard ½-inch cassette. In any event, there seems little doubt that the ¼-inch-tape videocassette recorder is not only here to stay but will become increasingly popular and more available.

THE TROUBLE WITH CABLE

Cable TV presents some special problems for VCRs. Chiefly because of the differences in the signals that are broadcast and received, it can be difficult—even impossible, under certain circumstances—to record one or more

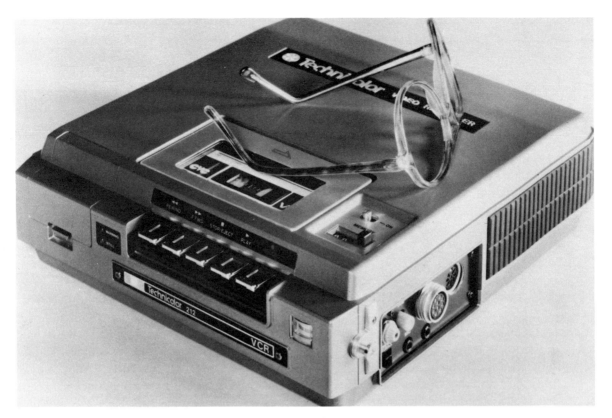

Technicolor's portable VCR features ¼-inch videotape, which is half the size of any other tape now available. It weighs only seven pounds, including battery. TECHNICOLOR, INC.

of the channels that are only available through the cable system. In other cases it may not be possible to record one channel while viewing another. There is a kind of Catch-22 operating here: There seems little point in bothering with video recording unless TV reception is excellent, but the best TV reception comes through a cable system that thwarts recording.

To record anything through a cable system it would be necessary to interconnect the VCR, the converter box provided by the cable company, and your TV set. If you connect the converter to the VCR and then hook up the VCR to the TV set, you will be able to record only the one channel that the channel selector on the converter points to. You will also have to watch that channel (unless, of course, you want to leave the room).

Alternatively, you could remove the connections from the cable to the converter box and hook the cable up to the VCR, then hook the VCR to the converter and, finally, connect the converter to your TV set. This will permit the programming and recording of the standard VHF channels (2 through 13) and any of the UHF channels that are being converted to standard VHF frequencies. This should enable you to record most cable TV programming, with the exception of the subscription TV channels (such as Home Box Office), which broadcast scrambled signals. A third possibility is perhaps a little easier but also more expensive and somewhat limiting. You can rent another converter box from the cable company and dedicate that to the VCR. You could then record through one converter box and watch TV through another. With this method, however, there is no automatic programming of the VCR, which will record only the channel on which its dedicated tuner has been set.

Recently several manufacturers have been offering special converters. (As was mentioned in Chapter 1, some new TV sets come equipped with such converters built in.) There are also special switching devices available which considerably simplify the process of switching the cable company's converter box from VCR to TV and back again. (These and other acessories are discussed in Chapter 9.)

WHEN SOMETHING IS WRONG

In view of the hefty price for even the most basic VCR, one would have a right to expect these machines to last for a long time and to function flawlessly during that time. Such expectations are, unfortunately, naive.

Probably the first thing to go on a VCR will be its heads. Most manufacturers agree that the recording and playing heads are good for a minimum of about one thousand hours. If one were to use a VCR nonstop, that would mean that the heads would begin breaking down in about six weeks. Obviously, almost no one uses a VCR in that manner. In general, those thousand hours should carry most users well beyond the first year of ownership. It will also carry most users well beyond the warranty period.

Service contracts are available, but they are not necessarily economical. (See my comments about service contracts in Chapter 1.) Typically, annual maintenance costs on a VCR are likely to run to about 20 percent of the original purchase price. This means that after five years a VCR owner is likely to have spent enough on maintenance and repairs to purchase a new machine—assuming, of course, that the ravages of inflation have not done their usual work.

One way to exacerbate wear and tear on the heads is to overwork the "pause" feature. During the pause mode, the recording or playback heads are still moving across the tape. The tape itself, however, is stationary. In other words, the heads are moving over the same area of tape for an extended period of time. Too long a pause, then, can cause damage to both heads and tape. If you purchase a VHS machine, you will have to take careful note of the maximum pause as given in the manufacturer's instruction manual. Beta systems are equipped to disengage the pause control automatically after four or five minutes.

Not everything that can go wrong with a VCR, however, can necessarily be blamed on the equipment. Human error is an all-too-frequent ingredient in unsuccessful VCR operations. For example, people have been known to misread the programming timer. Some VCRs have timers that indicate the programming days in numbers. Zero equals today, 1 equals tomorrow, 2 equals the day after tomorrow, and so forth. That would seem to be a relatively simple concept except for those who assume that 0 equals nothing and that 1 equals today, 2 means tomorrow, and so forth. The entire programming schedule can easily be set one full day off. According to consumer electronics writer Norman Schreiber, Sony models which indicate programming days as "today," "tomorrow," and "day after tomorrow" also cause problems. Schreiber, who has a keen eye for the absurd but (he has assured me) never lies, claims that people enter "today," "tomorrow," and so forth, either for the time they want to view the program rather than the time it should be recorded, or simply "today" because, as they explain it, "today is the day I entered the program." (*Video Review,* April 1980)

A VCR OPERATING CHECKLIST

Despite its multiplicity of functions, a VCR is relatively easy to operate once you get used to it. Nothing substitutes for practice, and after the first few attempts to get the system going, there should be little difficulty in keeping it running. If the machine doesn't seem to behave in a manner consistent with your commands, the problem may lie in one or more of the following situations and conditions:

1. If the "playback" or "record" control stubbornly refuses to stay down, it probably means that you have either forgotten to put a cassette in the machine or there is no more tape left on the cassette already in there. You will either have to rewind the cassette or replace it. Also, check your unit's dew light (sometimes called dewlamp). If the light is lit, it means there is moisture in your VCR, in which case you should either check the operating manual to see what to do next or, alternatively, leave the power on until the lamp goes out, signifying that the moisture has dried up.

2. If the "playback" and/or "record" buttons seem to be locked and will not operate at all, there could be four possible reasons.

A. Another control, such as "fast forward," is already pushed down. Press the "stop" button before proceeding.

B. There is no cassette in the machine. Either you forgot to put one in or someone removed the one you thought was in there when you were not looking.

C. The cassette is in there, but the cover of the cassette compartment has not been closed all the way to the locking position.

D. The "file/protect" tabs have been removed. If you look on the back of your cassettes, you will see small plastic tabs. (This is true of audio cassettes, too.) These can be removed to protect against accidental recording over material already on the cassette. Thus, you can play back the cassette but you cannot record; you will have to use another cassette to do so.

3. If the playback control functions but nothing else happens, there are five possible explanations.

A. Your TV set is tuned to an incorrect channel. Tune it to the channel that is required for playback—probably 3 or 4. (Check your machine's instruction manual.)

B. Check the cassette again. The one you put in the machine may be a blank.

C. Check to see whether the "pause" control is on. If it is, disengage it.

D. Your VCR has a "TV/cassette" or "TV/VCR" control. This control must be in the "TV" position for playback.

E. There may actually be a faulty connection between the VCR and the TV. Check the connectors to see that they are properly placed. If they are and everything else checks out, there may be a defect in the wiring.

4. If your VCR is in the "fast forward" or "rewind" mode and stops before the end of the tape is reached, you probably have the "memory" control on. Switch it off.

5. Perhaps one of the greatest frustrations inflicted upon modern humanity by modern technology is a VCR that fails to record the TV program its owner wanted it to record. There are five possibilities here.

A. The tuner on the VCR channel selector was set on a nonbroadcasting channel.

B. There is a problem with the fine tuning. Either it is not properly adjusted or the automatic fine tuner (AFT) button on the VCR was not pressed down.

C. You have forgotten to disconnect your video camera or microphone. Some VCR models will not record from TV sets when either of these is plugged in.

D. The "pause" control is still activated. Turn it off. If your VCR has a "camera/TV" or "camera/tuner" switch, that switch must be in the "tuner" or "TV" position for the VCR to record.

E. If all else fails, check the wiring and connections between the VCR and the TV set.

6. If, during ordinary TV viewing, the picture quality is poor or the color is nonexistent, the difficulty may lie in the VCR.

A. The "TV/cassette" or "TV/VCR" switch must be set on "TV."

B. The hookup between the TV and the VCR may be faulty. Check the connections.

C. The hookup between the TV antenna and the set may be faulty. To determine whether the problem is in the connection to the VCR or to the antenna, disconnect the antenna terminals from the VCR and hook them up to the TV set. If the picture improves, it is safe to assume that the problem is in the VCR.

D. Portable VCRs require an accessory tuner. If that tuner is not plugged into the electrical outlet, you will experience a poor and/or colorless picture.

7. If, on playback, the picture is marred by "snow" or streaks, there are five things to check.

A. The problem may lie with misalignment, wear, or just plain dirt on the recording/playback heads in the VCR. This will probably require servicing by a technician.

B. TV reception may have been poor during the recording because of a faulty antenna or poor connections between the antenna and the TV.

C. The fine tuning on the TV may have been off. Either the TV should have been better adjusted or the AFT control, where present, should have been engaged.

D. The problem may be in the cassette; specifically, there may be a worn or defective tape or one that has been badly recorded. This is easily checked by replacing the cassette that is giving the bad picture with one that you know plays back an acceptable image.

E. Check the tracking control on the VCR. It may require adjusting.

8. If portions of the picture near the top seem to bend or wave on playback, there are three explanations.

A. You may need to adjust the tracking control (a control that keeps the tape properly aligned on its tracks).

B. The tape may be defective.

C. An AFT circuit may be malfunctioning, particularly in older TV sets.

9. If, during playback, the picture vanishes for short periods of time, the solution to the problem may be out of your hands.

A. The tape may be worn or the entire cassette may be defective.

B. If it is a movie cassette, it may be a pirated tape made from an original that has been encoded for the precise purpose of thwarting such piracy. The cassette should be returned for refund or replacement.

10. If the picture rolls or "tears" during the playing of a commercial cassette, first check the horizontal and vertical controls on your TV set. (These are likely to be at the back of the set.) If that doesn't solve the problem, you probably have another cassette that has been pirated and subjected to encoding. Take it back to wherever it came from.

11. If the VCR fails to record from a video camera, check the following points.

A. Make sure all the connections are correctly and tightly made.

B. Make sure there is enough light. See if the camera lens opening has been properly set. It is impossible for light to enter the camera lens if you have forgotten to remove the lens cap. (We will have more to say about cameras in Chapter 8.)

C. Be certain that the camera itself has been turned on and has been given sufficient time to warm up.

D. Make sure that the "camera/tuner" control has been switched to "camera."

E. Make sure the "pause" control has been disengaged.

12. If the VCR fails to record the entire program for which it has been set, the problem invariably arises from an insufficiency of tape. Either the cassette that has been used does not have the capacity to record the full program or it has been partially used. Bear in mind that just because the tape counter has been set to zero, this is no guarantee that the tape itself will start at the beginning. It must be rewound.

13. Even after you have meticulously checked everything to make sure that all wires are properly hooked up, all controls are properly set, the cassette is exactly as it should be, and you look forward to coming home and finding that your favorite movie or TV show has been faithfully recorded, you nevertheless meet with disappointment. The machine has failed to record as programmed. In all probability there has been a power failure in your absence. (A quick check with a plugged-in electric clock in your home can tell you whether this is the case.) What makes the programming of a VCR possible is a tiny computer called a microprocessor, which has a "memory." A brief power failure, even one as short as fifteen seconds, can erase that memory.

Under the worst possible conditions, you will have carefully and thoroughly checked all the controls, connections, settings, determined that the electrical power is steady and constant, and still the VCR refuses to function. Before packing it up and shipping it off to the manufacturer or carting it back to the retailer or service company, check for one final flaw, the one that is by far the most common cause of all electronic failures: See whether your equipment has been plugged into the wall. Perhaps this sounds silly, patronizing, and maybe even a little insulting. If so, I apologize. The fact remains, however, that this is by all counts the single greatest reason for electrical and electronic equipment "failure."

Another cause of malfunction that is closely related to the one just mentioned has to do with cats, dogs, children, and other pets. An active creature moving about the house can, through carelessness, curiosity, or just plain mischief, pull out a plug, land on a switch or button, or in some other way rearrange and disarrange everything you have set up. The best advice, especially if you plan to let your VCR function in your absence, is to set everything in perfect working order, with proper programming and all the controls in place. Make sure everything is plugged in, make sure the power switch is on, and then *lock the room after you leave.*

Finally, remember that there is such a thing as being too careful. According to Norman Schreiber, "People have been known to turn a VCR power switch on, enter all the settings, double-check to see that everything is right, then turn the power off." The finest, most expensive, most efficient VCR in the world cannot function with the power switch off. These machines are capable of a wide range of operations; unfortunately, mind reading is not one of them.

BLANK CASSETTES

Videocassettes vary both in length of recording/playing time and in quality. These variations determine the price, which generally ranges from about $12 for a 30-minute cassette to about $26 for a 200-minute cassette. A little experimentation will determine which ones are best for your needs, both in terms of length and quality. For example, if you record something on a tape that you expect to keep for a very long time and intend to view with some frequency, you will probably want a fairly high-quality cassette. On the other hand, if you want to record some special event or program because you are unable to watch it during its normal broadcast time, but find that after you do see it you have no particular desire to see it again, a less expensive tape will probably suffice.

Obviously, the quality of the cassette itself will affect not only the quality of the mechanical performance but also the audio and video reproduction. There are a few basic rules to observe with respect to videocassettes. They are not very complicated and are worth adhering to for maximum longevity and quality of reproduction.

1. Begin with a quality cassette. Purchase a brand you know you can trust. Most of the well-known tape manufacturers supply cassettes for both VHS and Beta formats. There are a number of off-brand and bargain tapes available at highly attractive prices, but in the long run quality tapes are likely to prove more economical because they will last longer and will give a better performance. Among the well-known brands of videocassettes are:

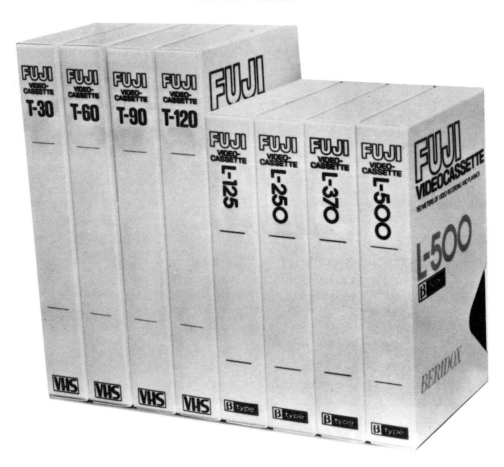

Most tape manufacturers offer a full line of videocassettes for both Beta and VHS formats.

FUJI PHOTO FILM USA INC., MAGNETIC TAPE DIV.

Akai, Ampex, BASF, DuPont, Fuji, GTE (Sylvania), Hitachi, JVC, Magnavox, Maxell, Memorex, Panasonic, Philco, Quasar, RCA, Sanyo, Sears, Sony, TDK, 3M, Toshiba, and Zenith.

Check the advertisements in the "Home" or "Entertainment" sections of your Sunday newspapers, as well as in the video magazines. Famous-brand tapes can often be purchased at extremely good prices through mail order firms.

2. Try not to drop or strike the cassette. Shocks can result in misalignments of the tape inside.

3. Too many sudden starts and stops during recording or playback should be avoided because they can stretch the tape. Stretching causes all sorts of problems with the picture.

4. The following point has been mentioned before, but it is worth repeating: Check the instruction manual that comes with your VCR for the maximum amount of time that the unit should be kept in the "pause" or "freeze-frame" mode. Avoid exceeding that time in order to prevent damage to both the cassette and the VCR.

5. Before putting away a cassette, "fast-forward" the tape to the end and then rewind it back to the beginning without stopping. This will rewind the tape smoothly and evenly and avoid stretching. It takes a few extra minutes, but it is well worth doing for the preservation of the tape.

6. Storing the cassettes in a vertical position also helps to prevent stretching by reducing pressure on the edges of the tape.

7. Dirt and dust can not only scratch the surface of the tape, thereby affecting video and audio quality, but can also cause damage to the VCR heads. The cassette should be replaced in its original sleeve before storing.

8. Avoid storing tapes in direct sunlight, in excessive heat, and in high humidity. The ideal storage temperature is between 60 and 70 degrees Fahrenheit, with a relative humidity of around 40 percent. (If the tape is subjected to extremely high temperature or humidity, store it in a cool, dry place for about 24 hours to allow the tape to return to normal before use.) Because the surface of the tape is magnetic, cassettes should be stored away from magnetic objects such as amplifiers, loudspeakers, and motors with large, permanent magnets. These magnets could easily erase portions of the tape. Usually a space of about 3 inches or more is enough to avoid any problems.

9. The VCR heads should be demagnetized periodically. This preserves both the tapes and the heads. There are several relatively low-cost devices for demagnetizing the heads. (These are discussed in Chapter 9.)

Incidentally, it is not easy to physically touch the tape inside a cassette, but some people consider it something of a challenge. It is a good idea to keep fingerprints off the tape because body oils attract and retain dust and dirt. Also, what applies to blank cassettes applies to commercially recorded or "prerecorded" cassettes. Once one owns a VCR, the purchase or rental of cassettes on which somebody else has made a recording seems inevitable.

PRERECORDED CASSETTES

When Sony introduced the first Betamax, the reaction of the entertainment industry was one of sheer pandemonium. Almost immediately Universal Pictures and Walt Disney Productions filed suit in court to have the Betamax declared illegal on the grounds that it was a device that would encourage the violation of copyright laws. The studios lost their suit (but have appealed); while they were fighting, several other film producers tiptoed, walked, or jumped headlong into the video business, primarily by licensing the reproduction on videotape of many of their major films. At the beginning of 1977 there were about sixty movie titles available on videocassettes. Within three years there were over five hundred such titles available, a growth of an incredible 854 percent. It seems as though everyone in the entertainment industry—film producers and distributors, television networks, publishers—is in the videocassette business in one way or another (not to mention the videodisc business, although we will mention it in the next chapter). Major motion pictures are available for purchase on cassettes at prices ranging anywhere from $35 to about $85. Videocassette shops are springing up all over the country, as are special videocassette sections in audio, camera, and department stores. In addition, films can be rented, borrowed, and exchanged. Nor are movies the only program material available on prerecorded cassettes. The National Video Clearinghouse, Inc., publishes three video tape/disc guides. The one on movies and entertainment covers "4,000 programs—all the great films, TV shows, concerts, and other entertainment features . . ." Their sports and recreation guide includes "1,000 programs on sports and outdoor activities—including great moments in sports, documentaries, instructional 'how-to' programs, and sports-related movies." The company's guide to children's programs contains "2,000 programs for children of all ages. Includes cartoons, young adult movies, educational and cultural features (hobbies, crafts, music, art, health, and social studies) . . ." (For more information on these excellent guides, write to the National Video Clearinghouse, Inc., 100 Lafayette Drive, Syosset, New York, 11791.) These guides are only an indication of the enormous variety of material already available and still to come on prerecorded videocas-

Many retailers who do not specialize in video —record stores, for instance—use displays like this one to sell videocassettes. ALLIED ARTISTS VIDEO CORP.

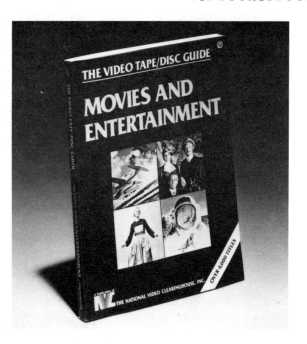

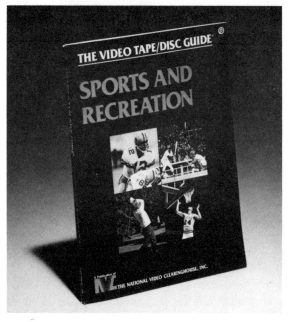

Various categories of video software are listed in these guides. THE NATIONAL VIDEO CLEARINGHOUSE, INC.

settes. Despite the fact that the cost of such cassettes seems high (Why would anyone want to spend as much as $85 to own a movie? How many times can you look at even your favorite movie?) there are apparently people who are willing to spend the money. Those who want to see the films but do not want to own them can rent cassettes for about $14 for a one-week period. Whether that is economical depends on how many people will be seeing the film during the rental period and what it would cost to take that many people to the movies.

I suppose I am duty-bound to point out that it is impossible to consider commercially available videocassettes for home entertainment without mentioning the vast quantity of pornographic material that is also available, ranging from reasonably high-quality films shown in movie theaters to the old-fashioned kind of black socks, fake nose, and mustache types filmed under a hundred-watt bulb in a motel room. There are some who believe that it was the availability of pornography that first gave VCRs their impetus. According to Chris Welles, "as much as sixty percent of pre-recorded video tape sales are pornographic films . . ." (*Esquire,* June 1980) I have neither the interest nor inclination to discuss the moral issues of pornographic films, nor would such a discussion be appropriate in this book. Your morality is your own business. I am here only to report on existing conditions. The purchase, rental, or exchange of pornographic material is simplicity itself. For one thing, almost any retail establishment that sells prerecorded videocassettes includes at least some pornography in its stock. Perhaps the easiest way to gain access to pornographic material, running the full gamut from very soft-core to raunchy/hard-core is to pick up a video magazine—any video magazine—at the newsstand, turn to the back, and begin flipping the pages. You will very soon come upon advertisements of X-rated videocassettes for sale or rent, the number and nature of which could easily make a less sophisticated person blush mightily.

Of course, such magazines also carry many advertisements for companies offering films of a somewhat more "legitimate" nature for sale. In addition, a variety of plans which work on the lending library principle or straight rental are available. These, too, advertise.

Companies that offer cassettes for sale or rent vary in size and variety of material. They also vary, apparently, in the longevity of their business lives. New ones seem to come and go every day. Perhaps the best way to find out what is currently available is to make a small investment in one or two magazines and mail a few postcards. By writing to the companies in the ads, you will soon be receiving thick catalogues with long lists of films in virtually every category and carrying ratings from G to XXX. Furthermore, you will probably have to do this only once. Given the propensity for selling and renting mailing lists, your name is likely to be bounced around the industry to such an extent that you will eventually incur the wrath and denunciation of your letter carrier.

VIDEO CLUBS

One way to avail yourself of a variety of types of cassettes and an ever-changing program of entertainment and instruction in your home is to join a video club. Most clubs are subsidiaries of other companies. They operate in a manner similar to book clubs, except that you do not automatically receive cassettes; you have to specifically order the ones you want. The clubs all have membership fees which entitle members to regularly published periodicals that give titles and descriptions of available cassettes. The members may then order the titles for relatively low fees, with the understanding that the cassettes will be returned within a specified period of time. (*Note:* There is no "negative option" feature with most video clubs. Negative option is the euphemism that book clubs and other mail-order operators use to describe the situation where you do nothing if you want what is being offered that month. Stated another way, if you do not want to receive the offering, you must so inform the club.) Unlike book clubs, video clubs usually have no minimum ordering requirements.

If you are considering joining a video club, shop around as you would for anything else. Watch for things like low one-time or annual membership fees that are compensated for by higher rental prices. Also watch for instances where the rental or purchase price seems to be extremely low but does not include postage and handling. This could add anywhere from $2 to $5 to the cost of each cassette.

The following is a random sampling of video clubs. Many more exist and can be found in the video magazines.

American Video Tape Library, 6200 South Broadway, Littleton, Colorado 80121. This club began as a nonprofit organization. For a one-time fee (about $90) plus low monthly dues (about $5) members may borrow as many cassettes as they wish—but only one at a time.

Time-Life Video Club, Harrisburg, Pennsylvania 17105. This club functions very much like a conventional book club. There is a one-time membership fee of $15 and cassettes are offered at approximately 20 percent below retail price. This club offers special features, such as the excellent Time-Life films.

The Video Club of America, P.O. Box D, Madison Heights, Michigan 48071. This club is a subsidiary of Twentieth Century-Fox and claims to be the largest producer of prerecorded videocassettes. There is a lifetime membership fee of $25 and the club offers premiums with movies that are ordered.

VidAmerica, 235 E. 55th Street, New York, New York 10022. This is a rental and purchase club that asks a $10 membership fee (which is refunded with the purchase of an accessory) and rents programs for a seven-day period for prices ranging from about $10 to $14. At present, the club requires a deposit of $50 for each program rented unless transactions are made by credit card. A monthly program guide is mailed to all members.

Inovision, P.O. Box 40040, 1250 American Parkway, Dallas, Texas 75234. The dues of $12 per year entitle members to select from a large list of programs that are available for one-week rentals, with prices ranging from about $9 to about $11. Occasionally members of Inovision are also offered discounts on a wide range of video, stereo, computer, and other electronic equipment and products.

VCRs AND THE LAW

When Walt Disney Productions and Universal Pictures sued Sony for copyright infringement, they were raising the question as to whether the recording of copyrighted material was a violation of the copyright laws. The initial decisions seemed to indicate that there is no such copyright infringement. Nevertheless, a number of legal questions remain. These issues are extremely complex; at this writing they are still being argued and decided. It will probably be years before definitive decisions are reached about what is or is not legal. Among the complications are the fact that judges in different jurisdictions have been known to hand down opposing decisions in cases that appear to be similar.

For those reasons, and because I have neither the qualifications nor the authority to do so, this book cannot offer any legal advice. I would like to suggest, however, two good rules of thumb: First, if you think something may be illegal, don't do it. Second, if you are planning to use a prerecorded videocassette or a videocassette recording of a commercial TV program for a public showing, especially one where money will be collected (even if it is for a charitable or nonprofit purpose), get a friendly lawyer to look over the fine print in your club agreement or the statement packed with the prerecorded cassette you purchased.

In general, you can record programs coming in over the cable and off the air for your personal use. You can probably also record special cable or pay TV shows for your home and personal use unless there is a clause in the contract with the local cable company that restricts your recording rights.

But what about going beyond your own personal use? Can you, for example, exchange tapes with another individual without running afoul of the law? The answer here is somewhat iffy. According to one attorney, "While we cannot tell you unconditionally that there is no risk of being sued in a civil proceeding by a copyright owner for such lending or exchanging, we do feel, as a practical matter, that there is little likelihood of such a suit being initiated or successfully pursued." (Jim Lowe, *Video Review,* April 1980) Apparently, then, practicality is as much a factor as legality. What purpose would be solved by a company suing you for swapping tapes with a friend?

There are a number of operators throughout the country selling bootleg or pirated VCR material, especially feature films. It is a simple matter, using even basic home VCR units, to purchase or rent a film through regular channels and then make copies of it. If you purchase one of these bootleg copies, you run two risks. First, because originals tend to be encoded for the express purpose of avoiding such bootlegging, you may wind up with a cassette that you will be unable to watch. Second, if the copyright owner decides to file suit, which in this case would probably be a criminal action, that owner would probably have the right to confiscate the tape, although the purchaser would probably not otherwise be involved in the proceedings—unless, of course, the purchaser had made the purchase with the direct intent of reselling the bootleg videotape.

There is no predicting when all of the legal matters will be clarified. The so-called "Betamax suit" is being appealed and predictions are that it will reach the U. S. Supreme Court somewhere around 1982 or 1983. In the meantime, Congress may pass appropriate legislation that more clearly defines the legal rights and obligations with respect to copyrighted video material and its purchase, sale, and exchange.

In the meantime, let the big corporations and their expensive lawyers have their fun in and out of the courts. You can have yours in your living room, not only by watching and using your VCR, but, when video begins to pall, by watching the infighting that goes on in the industry. If you think the entertainment industry is falling all over itself to achieve a standing in the videocassette market, you should see what is happening in videodiscs.

5

Videodiscs

You have added worth unto't and lustre,
And entertain'd me with mine own device . . .

—Timon of Athens, I, ii

As Christmas approached, the good citizens of Atlanta, Georgia, awoke one morning in 1978 to the happy discovery that to all of the multifarious products and wares available to bestow on others or themselves as part of the holiday largesse there was added yet another: Magnavision. Magnavision was, and is, a videodisc system offering many of the advantages of a VCR, plus a few of its own, and none of the disadvantages. As the new year progressed, Magnavision became available in a few additional test markets. Thus it was that the Magnavox Consumer Electronics Company gave birth in the marketplace to yet another technological miracle—and its inevitable result: a monumental marketing war.

A videodisc system is designed to play back material that has been prerecorded. In princi-

ple it is as easy to play a videodisc as it is to play a phonograph record. There are only two basic components to the system: the player which resembles the typical ubiquitous audio record player and is about the size of a compact stereo system; and the disc itself, which, not surprisingly, resembles an ordinary 12-inch record. The player is hooked up to a TV set through the antenna terminals. The technology can deliver sights and sounds never before obtainable through an ordinary TV set.

Almost from the very beginning, it seemed that Magnavision was going to be a huge success. The videodisc players cost less than VCRs and all that would be necessary would be for Magnavox to license other companies to manufacture machines under its system

Magnavision was the first videodisc player on the market. It uses a laser optical viewing system. Its features include fast, normal, slow, and still in forward position; normal, slow, and still in reverse position; variable speed control; reverse and forward search; and choice of stero sound or bilingual programming. MAGNAVOX CONSUMER ELECTRONICS CO.

and to permit record manufacturers to produce the discs. Everyone involved would get a generous slice of the consumer pie. But such is not the nature of the consumer electronics industry.

With considerable pre-marketing ballyhoo, RCA introduced its rival product, SelectaVision, in March 1981. SelectaVision was promoted as being considerably cheaper to produce and maintain than the Magnavox system. Thus, in a replay of the rivalry between the Beta and VHS videocassette systems, electronic history seems to be repeating itself.

The Magnavox system is an *optical* system. It uses a laser beam to pick up the information encoded on the disc. Among the advantages of this system is that nothing actually touches the surface of the disc; a single frame can be viewed for very long periods without causing any wear and tear. Furthermore, the optical system's disc turns at 1800 revolutions

per minute (rpm), a speed which provides excellent picture and sound quality.

RCA's SelectaVision is a *capacitance* system. Here, too, the discs are encoded, but a diamond stylus "reads" the information in the grooves. The RCA discs move at 450 to 1800 rpm. Capacitance is defined as "the ability to store an electric charge." The SelectaVision's stylus is sensitive to the variations of electrical charges stored in the grooves of the disc.

Thus, we now have two systems: the optical, also known as the VLP (video long play), and the capacitance, also known as CED (capacitance electronic disc).

Apart from the internal workings of the machines, the major differences, as far as the consumer is concerned, have to do with price and longevity. The optical systems sell for about $800. RCA's capacitance system costs about $525. (Discs for both systems cost about the same—between $20 and $25 for a

*The Magnavision videodisc player, with a disc
in place.* MAGNAVOX CONSUMER ELECTRONICS
CO.

*RCA's SelectaVision videodisc player, the
major competition for Magnavision.* RCA,   CONSUMER ELECTRONICS.

full-length motion picture.) Discs for the optical system are never touched and could presumably last indefinitely, whereas the RCA-type discs are predicted to have an effective life of about a hundred hours. That, however, can be a very long time. Each disc (in all systems) contains about two hours of playing time. A single disc would have to be played a great many times to total one hundred hours and reach the point where it fails to deliver a satisfactory picture.

Thus, while it would appear that electronic history involving the rivalry between the Beta and VHS VCRs is repeating itself in videodiscs, this is not quite true; there is a third player in the disc drama.

JVC (Victor Company of Japan) and Panasonic have introduced yet another version of the capacitance-type system. It is called the *video high density/audio high density* (VHD/AHD) system. As with the RCA system, this product uses a 10-inch disc contained in a plastic sleeve. The sleeve and its contents are inserted into the player. It, too, has a two-hour playing time capability. The main differences are that the VHD discs are grooveless, revolve at 900 rpm, and are reported to be able to last through more than 100,000 plays. Instead of a conventional stylus the VHD system uses an electrode made of sapphire or diamond. Instead of grooves this system uses "pits" engraved on the surface of the disc. The electrode moves over the pits but does not come in direct contact with them. This system claims to offer a number of the capabilities of RCA's system: freeze-frame, slow motion, and rapid reverse and forward action. (RCA's first models are expected to offer only high speed picture search.)

It should come as no surprise to learn that the three systems are completely incompatible. Furthermore, several other types of systems are in existence. Some of them appeared in Europe as early as 1975 and others are reportedly in the works but are not yet on the market. In general, most marketing forecasters are banking on the predominance of the optical and capacitance systems, with the two variations of the latter.

Magnavision has already demonstrated the potential of a good videodisc system. It can do almost anything a VCR can do—and can even do some of those things better. In addition to offering extremely high-quality pictures and sound, the videodisc makes it possible to randomly and rapidly access any particular point on the disc. The program can be played at slower or higher speeds and in both forward and reverse modes. The advantages of such a system are obvious. Imagine a disc that shows the techniques of a champion tennis player. Every motion, position, and nuance of style and technique could be scrutinized with no difficulty and studied for long periods of time.

Each disc is capable of recording 54,000 frames per side of full-screen display of information. Theoretically, the contents of an enormous number of books could be stored on a single videodisc. It is conceivable that one or two videodiscs could easily hold the entire Oxford English Dictionary, complete with supplements. These machines are capable of coding and cross-referencing each frame. It then becomes convenient, easy, and undoubtedly faster to look up a word on a disc than in a book on a shelf.

Still, if the promotional material is to be believed, there are certain advantages to the RCA system. Chief among them, of course, is the cost. Second, the system itself is fairly compact and occupies less space than the optical system. Also, it is supposedly easier to repair and maintain with standard replacement parts, as compared to the rather complicated and sophisticated optical videodisc system.

It remains to be seen whether one of the three systems will eventually dominate. In all likelihood, each will cling to a substantial chunk of the market. As for the software, again, videocassette history will probably be repeated with the videodisc. Those producers not aligned with any of the companies manu-

The third and latest entry into the videodisc free-for-all is the VHD system, developed by JVC and Panasonic Company. PANASONIC CO.

facturing the machines will probably be turning out discs for all three systems. This precedent has been established not only in VCRs but in audio recording, where a great many programs are available on long-playing discs, audio cassettes, and 8-track cartridges. The relative ease and economy of reproducing a videodisc (supposedly they can be duplicated at a cost of about $1 each) also makes it easier to work around the obstacle of three separate formats.

The fact remains that videodiscs are expected to become a major home-entertainment medium by the mid-1980s. Many companies are already heavily committed, financially and philosophically, to marketing and producing videodiscs and players. The enormous potential of this market becomes clear when one considers the number of audio records sold, especially to young people, who so far have been content only to listen to the music. Imagine how much more readily these same purchasers will snap up records that not only give them music but pictures too—and for approximately the same price.

Major corporations recognize this potential. We are seeing some rather strange and pre-

viously unheard-of commercial alliances. For the first time in its history, for example, International Business Machines (IBM) has moved heavily into the consumer market by buying into DiscoVision, the marketing arm for optical software, which originally consisted of a corporate combination involving Magnavox and its parent, the Dutch electronics colossus N. V. Philips, and MCA, the entertainment giant. Each of the major networks, most major motion picture producers, and, of course, the record companies are either deeply involved, or have announced plans for involvement, in the production and distribution of videodiscs. Some of the alliances are strange indeed. For example, who would have thought that CBS would have anything to do with NBC? Nevertheless, as part of its enormous marketing push in advance of actually selling any videodisc players, NBC's parent, RCA, has joined forces with CBS. The latter has promised to begin manufacturing its own SelectaVision videodiscs by 1982. In the meantime, discs with the CBS label are being turned out by RCA manufacturing facilities. Zenith, another of RCA's arch-rivals in the marketing of TV sets, has also joined in a

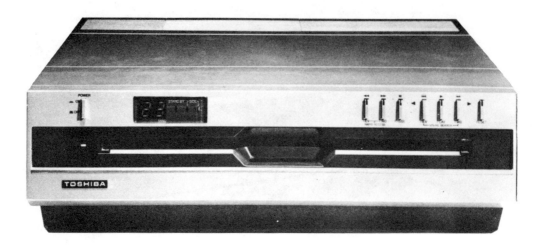

Several manufacturers are producing players compatible with the RCA system. TOSHIBA AMERICA, INC.

partnership. Zenith expects to begin manufacturing its own capacitance videodisc players sometime in the early 1980s; until then the company will market its own brand of players that have been manufactured by RCA. RCA has signed agreements with some twenty European and Japanese (Toshiba, Hitachi, Sanyo) companies to license production of its SelectaVision-type units.

These electronic giants are fighting over what is expected to be a very sizable chunk of territory. Every American home with a TV set is considered a potential customer for a videodisc system. Prognosticators predict that VCRs and videodisc players will not only not compete but will actually enhance each other's sales. RCA has projected a total revenue for the videodisc industry of $7.5 billion annually.

Here, then, is a breakdown of the various characters and the roles they are playing. Bear in mind that more members are likely to be added to the cast, roles are almost certain to shift, and—who knows?—some new technology may change the entire scenario.

Optical videodisc systems (VLP). Companies who have indicated their commitment to this system include Magnavox, Pioneer, and Gold Star.

Grooved capacitance systems (CED). So far, RCA, Zenith, Sears, and J. C. Penney have promised to begin marketing videodiscs using this system.

Grooveless capacitance systems (VHD). General Electric, Quasar, Panasonic, and JVC will be banking on this system.

Still to be heard from at this writing are Sony, Sharp, Philco, MGA/Mitsubishi, and Curtis Mathes.

SOFTWARE

According to *Stereo Review,* the catalogue of discs that will be available for playing on the SelectaVision system will consist of some three hundred programs. About half of these will be devoted to sports, music, children's programs, ballet, and so forth. The remaining half will consist of feature-length films. Each of the discs will have the maximum two hours' playing time and will sell for from $15 to $20.

With the enormous capacity for storage, the potential for variety and versatility on videodiscs is staggering. Imagine seeing all of *Swan Lake,* performed by Rudolph Nureyev and Margot Fonteyn, in your living room for a set of discs costing about $20—the price of an ordinary audio disc providing only the music. In fact, DiscoVision, which distributes the Magnavox discs, has just such a package.

Videodiscs also have an enormous industrial and commercial potential. With their ability to store huge amounts of information in a small space, they could significantly change such areas as office filing systems, commercial and industrial training programs, and could eventually revolutionize storage media in the computer field. The major obstacle here is the inability of the owner to "write" on a blank disc. Evolving technology will probably change that in the foreseeable future. In the meantime, a number of companies are already demonstrating that it is useful to have discs custom-made for them. The consumer disc slot that IBM has moved into was vacated by MCA, which has now given itself over exclusively to the production of videodiscs for General Motors. GM now owns over ten thousand specially designed optical videodisc players, which have been installed in dealers' showrooms as an efficient and effective technique for demonstrating GM cars and trucks.

Another likelihood is that videodisc players will be used for audio recordings as well. The technique of digitally recording material that is used in videodiscs allows for extremely high-quality sound reproduction. The Pioneer videodisc player is already equipped with a plug-in jack that accepts the decoding unit required to play such discs through existing hi-fi systems. (The decoder itself, however, is still on the technological horizon.)

As we have seen, videodisc players offer almost everything VCRs offer. Their main disadvantage is that they can only reproduce prerecorded material. They do not have the capability of making home productions or recording off-the-air programs. (Conceivably, with a little electronic hooking up, one could transfer material from a videodisc to a videotape.) Owning a VCR does not preclude owning a videodisc player, and vice versa. Many people already recognize the convenience—and sometimes the necessity—of having phonograph records and a tape recorder at the same time. The same conveniences that obtain for audio recording and playback are likely to hold true for video recording and playback.

The prospects, then, for the videodisc industry and for the consumer are enormous. So are the prospects for problems. By the end of 1980 one of the country's largest retailers of records and electronic products was already claiming that anywhere from 10 to 50 percent of the videodiscs purchased were defective. Nevertheless, according to a company executive, purchasers are "committed to the product" and are "cool about it so long as we are willing to make an exchange."

The question, finally, is: Should you be "committed to the product" as well? As is stated elsewhere in this book, it has generally been my philosophy that if you want it or need it and can afford it, then buy it. For once, however, it is probably wise to deviate from that philosophy somewhat. This is being written just after the RCA SelectaVision appeared on the market. Despite all of RCA's market research, promises, and projections, it is the consumer who will ultimately decide whether SelectaVision is a success. That is true, of course, for all the other videodisc systems as well. (For one thing, retailers have told me that while much of the software has been promised, precious little is actually available.) In the meantime, giants such as Sony, Sylvania, and Mitsubishi are yet to be heard from. Unless you have an unquenchable desire to squander a few hundred dollars, it is probably best to hold off for a little while before investing in a videodisc player. Should you succumb to temptation, you will probably not be terribly bad off. On the other hand, if you want a videodisc player because time hangs heavy on your hands, there are plenty of other things to do.

You could, for example, play a few video games.

6

Video Games

Away! the gentles are at their game, and we will to our recreation.

—*Love's Labour's Lost,* IV, ii

A significant proportion of what manufacturers and merchants like to refer to as "the consumer electronics industry" owes its existence to computer technology. The first practical computer consisted of a conglomeration of lights, wires, and a seemingly endless number of vacuum tubes. Beginning with the development of the transistor in the late 1950s by researchers at Bell Laboratories, miniaturization and, eventually, subminiaturization began replacing the tubes with smaller and more efficient circuitry.

In 1969 M. E. Hoff, Jr., an engineer for Intel Corporation, a company that manufactured circuitry chips, undertook a project involving the production of calculators for a Japanese manufacturer. In the process, Mr. Hoff discovered that he could incorporate the entire central processing unit (the "brains") of a computer on a single silicon chip. Silicon is a semiconductor; that is, a material which carries or conducts electricity in ways that can be chemically controlled. The circuitry is etched into the chip through a technique very similar to photoengraving, beginning with a master drawing that is reduced about five hundred times. The result is some highly complex circuitry on a chip about the size of a human fingernail.

By reducing the size of these control units, called *microprocessors,* it has become possible to manufacture, at almost laughably low cost, such niceties as digital watches with multiple functions and hand-held calculators capable of performing operations that once required a computer large enough to fill a room. Calcu-

Members of the Sonoma, California, State University's Space Invaders (trademark of Taito America Corporation) Club work out on Atari's Video Computer System home video game in preparation for the First Atari Space Invaders/Breakout National Championships.

The "Space Invaders" craze has inspired songs, T-shirts, and clubs such as this one, which ranks its members according to points scored in the game. (players, l. to r.: Butch Hoover, Sue Strader, Dave Smeds, Karen Escalera, George Lewis). ATARI, INC.

lators and digital watches *are,* in fact, small computers.

Certain information, or *programs,* are stored electronically in the microprocessor. In calculators, for example, the calculator must "know" how to perform the various mathematical functions required to provide the information you need. In other words, a microcomputer is capable of taking the information you give it and "processing" it (hence the term data processing) in the proper sequence in order to give you the proper answer.

If this technology can be employed to determine time lapses, or set off an alarm on your wrist, or deliver square roots and metric conversions in a calculator, it should also be pos-sible to use it for fun and games. It is. The microprocessor is at the heart of video games.

Video games have been around for some time. The first of these for home use was "Odyssey," produced and sold by Magnavox in 1972. These and several competitive lines achieved only limited popularity.

Some companies, however, preferred another direction. Instead of, or in addition to, producing games for home use, they supplied game arcades in amusement parks and other areas with games employing electronics and microprocessors. By 1974 nearly two dozen companies were selling coin-operated video games. Although they were called video games, the nomenclature was essentially an acknowledgment of the fact that they included a TV-like screen that was "dedicated"—that is, it was used for no other videonic purpose. One of the most popular of these games was "Pong," by Atari, Inc. "Pong" was, in essence, the foundation on which Atari built its current leadership in the video games industry.

By 1975 technology had evolved to the point where a microprocessor chip that sold for about $6 could be programmed for six different games. This innovation gave new life to the home video game market, and a number of manufacturers began producing games that could easily be played through the home TV set. (At about that time, so-called hand-held video games also began appearing; these, too, have steadily gained in popularity as technology continues to improve and prices continue to be reduced or remain stable. Strictly speaking, however, these hand-held games, while they are videolike, are not played on the home TV screen. Having acknowledged their existence, therefore, we shall abandon them for the rest of this discussion.)

In the meantime, arcade games also continued to gain in popularity until, almost inevitably, at least one game became something of a craze. In 1978 a game called "Space Invaders" was introduced to Japan by Taito, Inc. Within a year, over 100,000 "Space Invaders" machines were happily devouring well over $600 million throughout the country. The Bank of Japan was forced to triple its production of 100-yen coins to satisfy the insatiable "Space Invaders" players. When Bally Manufacturing Company introduced the coin-operated game to American arcades, whole new populations of fanatics flocked to the amusement centers.

In 1980 Atari, Inc., a part of the Warner Communications conglomerate, obtained exclusive rights to market the home video version of "Space Invaders" in the United States. Before the year was half over, Atari was claiming that "Space Invaders" had become the fastest selling of the forty-two games the company currently markets for home video.

As that last sentence implies, "Space Invaders" is by no means the only game in town, nor is Atari the only dealer. There are scores of games available, and what makes them so popular is that while some of them may be rather complicated to play and offer varying degrees of challenge to players' skills, they are relatively easy to install.

In most instances a master control unit hooks up to the TV set through the antenna terminals. The software—the program for the game itself—is contained in a cartridge which is inserted into the master unit. Each cartridge contains a different game and not all games, even within the same system, necessarily operate by means of the same controls. There are various kinds of push buttons and key pads, joysticks (which resemble little versions of the steering control in aircraft), and dials or knobs. Once the master control unit is installed, it can usually be left in place; it is not necessary to disconnect the game to watch television or to use other video equipment.

It is probably possible, through some careful wiring or the use of one of the switching devices described in Chapter 9, to record the playing of a video game on a VCR for instant replay. Why anyone would want to do such a thing, however, is beyond me. The only way to improve one's skill in a video game is to keep playing it until one has either mastered it or reached the limits of one's own ability. I can see nothing to be gained by taping the action, and anyone who would videotape his or her own game-playing to show others would be guilty of perpetrating one of the most torturously boring activities since the invention of home movies.

Perhaps one of the more discouraging aspects of video games is that many of them seem to be nothing more than variations on the same basic theme. Something moves across the screen and you are supposed to hit it, capture it, destroy it, or in some other way make contact with it. It is, essentially, a matter of the electronics controlling one blip

This popular video game system shows the wide variety of games available. Note the ease with which game cartridge fits into unit. This photo also illustrates (l. to r. foreground) joysticks, key pads, and dial controls. ATARI, INC.

while the player controls another. These games are primarily tests of skill and reaction time. It does not matter whether there are battleships being struck by torpedoes, airplanes being brought down by antiaircraft missiles, or some blip or representation thereof being struck by some other blip or representation thereof.

Fortunately, with the increasing sophistication of the technology and of the video game player, the notion of hitting one blip with another has been made considerably more complicated and interesting. In addition, a number of familiar and standard games can be played on the home video screen, including chess, checkers, backgammon, baseball, football, and others.

Also typical of video games is the fact that they can be programmed for various levels of difficulty to either sharpen and develop the skills of the player or to accommodate players with varying degrees of skill. A good video chess game, for example, should be able to provide a challenge for the resident eight-year-old, as well as for his or her older siblings and parents. (This assumes, of course, that the resident eight-year-old is not already demolishing his older siblings and parents, in which case the video game can be used to improve one's game in the hope of eventually putting the little smart aleck in his or her place.)

Many games now deliver sound effects along with the action. You can enjoy the real-

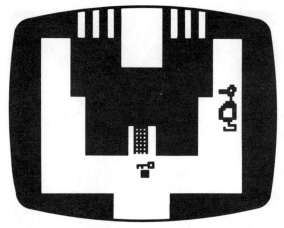

ADVENTURE Game Program™

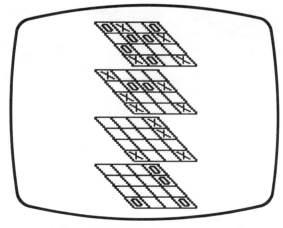

3-D TIC-TAC-TOE Game Program™

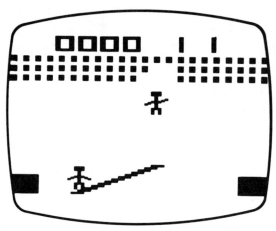

CIRCUS ATARI Game Program™

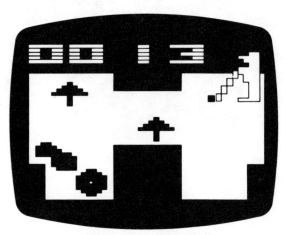

GOLF Game Program™

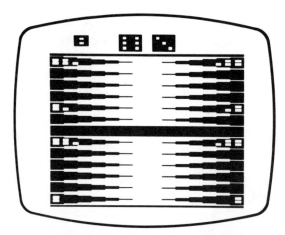

BACKGAMMON Game Program™

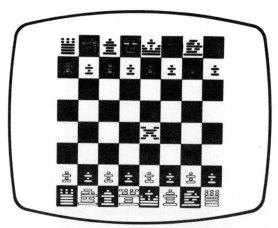

VIDEO CHESS™ Game Program™

SUPERMAN* Game Program™
*SUPERMAN is the trademark of and   DC Comics, Inc. 1979

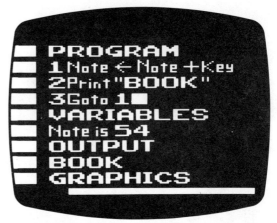

BASIC PROGRAMMING Game Program™

Examples of some typical video games and how they appear on the TV screen. ATARI, INC.

ism of explosions, heavy artillery, the roar of crowds at the races, the arena, the shuffling of cards in the casino, and other interesting noises.

Obviously, the cost of video games varies significantly with the sophistication of the system and the software. For example, a fairly inexpensive system is the Telstar Colortron by Coleco. It includes tennis, hockey, jai alai, and handball. All four games can be played by two players. The system sells for about $25, but it does not accept any other game cartridges and no other games can be played with it. At the other end of the scale is the Atari Video Computer System, which retails for about $200 and offers over forty cartridges, ranging in price from $22 to $38. There are many variations within the cartridges. For example, the "Video Olympics" cartridge has a fifty-game program. The company's version of the ubiquitous "Space Invaders" offers over a hundred different ways of playing the game.

Atari's most serious challenger appears to be Mattel, the toy manufacturer. This company recently introduced Intellivision, which has a suggested retail price of $300 but which offers, in addition to an array of games, two important innovations. First, the company promises that by the end of 1981 Intellivision

owners will be able to obtain over a dozen new cartridges each month, at a cost of around $10 each, through their local cable TV companies. More significant, however, is the fact that Intellivision is already equipped to accept a typewriterlike keyboard that will convert the unit to a relatively simple home computer. If the company's promises are to be believed, that keyboard should be available by the time you read this. If guesses and predictions are accurate, it should be selling for $500 or $600.

As has been indicated, there is a wide variation in the number and kinds of games available, as well as in their costs. Furthermore, video game producers are continually adding to their lines. It would be futile, therefore, to attempt to summarize, with any degree of accuracy, the number and kinds of games available. Once again it is a good idea to rely on one of the video magazines to keep you up-to-date as to what is available, at what cost, and, significantly, at what discounts.

BUYING VIDEO GAMES

In general, there are several factors that should be considered when one is shopping for a video game.

Challenge. Unless you enjoy looking at the

The keyboard shown here is actually an add-on accessory that turns the game system into a *personal computer.* INTELLIVISION™, MATTEL ELECTRONICS, DIV. OF MATTEL, INC.

patterns on the screen, there seems little point in purchasing a video game that is too easy to play or that quickly becomes boring. Similarly, there seems no point in bucking a game that is beyond your capacities. The ideal video game offers a challenge that you are capable of meeting, at least eventually, and then goes on to offer still greater accomplishments.

Graphics. The images and symbols on the screen should be clear, colorful, and easy to recognize and differentiate. You cannot play a game very well if you cannot recognize the players or the playing field.

Controls. Since so many video games depend on responsiveness and dexterity, your own responsiveness and dexterity should not be frustrated by controls that are awkward or difficult to operate. That applies, of course, to other family members as well. Key pads and push buttons should be easy to get to and

should fit the hands of all who are expected to participate.

Variety. Shooting down blips, whether they look like battleships or airplanes, can quickly become boring. If you can afford it, look for a system that either accepts additional cartridges with more games or that has several variations of the games that are built in. You may want to play blackjack on one day and backgammon on another. Both are available in home video games, but not necessarily in the same system.

Service. I have said it before and I will say it again: Check the warranty. Make sure your system is backed by an adequate warranty. Also make sure that the servicing facilities are relatively convenient. If you have to mail or ship the unit to a factory-service facility, you may want to begin with a unit that is readily shippable.

"Odyssey 2" is the latest version of one of the pioneering video game systems. MAGNAVOX CONSUMER ELECTRONICS CO.

Versatility. Some systems offer more than just games. Atari, for example, offers a $40 cartridge that teaches basic computer programming. Other cartridges offer various educational games and programs for such subjects as mathematics, foreign languages, and so forth.

Creativity. Some systems enable the user to create his or her own games and store them on an audiotape cassette that is recorded and played back through an audio tape recorder. (More about this shortly.)

Modularity. You may want to gradually add on to your home video game system. Some systems allow separate purchase of ad-

ditional controls, various kinds of converters and switches, and other accessories to expand the system.

Home video game systems are not cheap. The price, however, has to be measured in something more than the dollars-and-cents outlay for the cost of the system and its cartridges. Many video game players and their families are staying home more and playing games together. Apart from the social benefits of such activity, there are considerable savings in the areas of fuel, parking, admission prices to outside amusements, and babysitters. De-

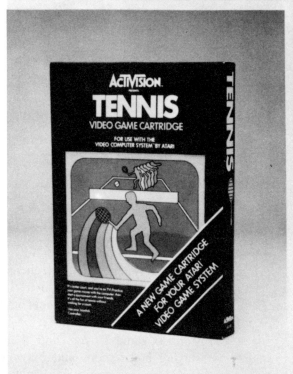
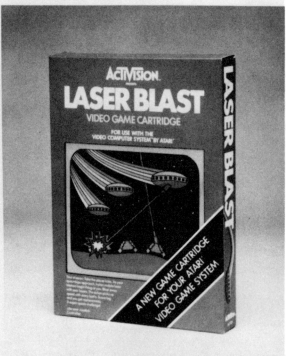

At least one company is providing software for video game systems manufactured by another firm. These cassettes are among an extensive line produced exclusively for Atari system owners. ACTIVISION INC.

pending upon the number of people using them and the frequency with which they are being used, video games can, in the long run, actually cost a good deal less than they might appear to at first.

MORE SOFTWARE

One company has recently initiated what is probably going to become a trend. ActiVision Inc., of Sunnyvale, California, is now producing several video games that are compatible with the Atari system. As in other areas of home video, it seems likely that independent software producers will choose up sides, determine which of the dominating systems they want to align themselves with, and then produce software for that system.

Already the field has its experts and critics. One Thomas Corbett, age nineteen, has developed a video game rating system. He awards chips, ranging from one chip for "no fun" to six chips for "hyperfun." (*Panorama,* November 1980.)

PROGRAMMING YOUR OWN GAMES

To program your own games, you need "input," in other words, some means of putting information into the system. Typically, this medium is a keyboard, either of the typewriter type or of the key pad type, similar to the arrangement of push buttons on a telephone or a hand-held calculator. You will also need some kind of storage medium, such as an audiotape cassette. Also required is "memory" —a means for the game system to remember how the game is to be played. You will also need "output"—something on which to receive the information that comes out of the system. In this case, the output is your video screen. Finally, in order to do all of this "talking" to the system, you need to speak its language, generally something called BASIC, the simplest of computer languages. When you are finished, what you have, essentially, is a computer that plays games.

The next logical step, then, is a computer that does more than just play games.

7

Home Computers

O excellent device! was there ever heard a better . . . ?

—*The Two Gentlemen of Verona,* II, i

As we have just seen, some game systems can be more or less upgraded to function as simple computers. Conversely, virtually any computer can be used for, among other things, game-playing.

As I said earlier, one of the more remarkable characteristics of the electronics industry is that in an era of rapidly rising inflation, prices for electronic devices have either remained stable or have actually been dramatically reduced. Nowhere is this more evident than in the field of computers. It is as true for the monstrous, complex systems of major corporations and governments as it is for small, compact units, aptly referred to as microcomputers, for personal and home use. Indeed, so sophisticated and efficient are some of these machines that the phrase home computer is

somewhat limiting. These computers are showing up more and more in small businesses and in professional offices, where they are performing a number of important business and management functions. One of the chief attractions of personal computers is that they can be easily connected to a home television set. But there is more than a TV screen to a computer.

THE BASIC COMPUTER

Every computer consists of five basic components: input, a central processing unit, memory, storage, and output.

Input. This is a device or medium for putting information into the computer. Typically, it is some kind of keyboard, either *alphanu-*

The Atari 800™ Personal Computer System.   ATARI, INC.

meric (i.e., a typewriterlike keyboard that has all the letters of the alphabet, the digits 0 through 9, and some special signs or symbols), or a key pad that has only the digits plus a few special signs. The key pad on a push-button telephone functions, in many applications, as input for computers.

Central processing unit (CPU). Here is where the actual computation is done. In personal computers and many smaller business computers the entire CPU is contained on a chip of silicon. The CPU itself holds the circuitry through which the actual processing of data is performed. (*Note:* If a lack of interest has caused you to bypass the chapter on video games, I suggest you go back and read the first few pages to understand a little more about silicon chips and subminiaturization.)

Memory. When you place information into a computer, the system must hold on to that information long enough to process it. Thus, if you want your hand-held calculator to multiply 147 by 382, it must retain those numbers until you tell it what to do with them. The facility to temporarily store electronically the information you put into a computer is called its memory.

Storage. Storage is very similar to memory except that it tends to hold more permanent information. Thus, while memory will temporarily retain the numbers you want to multiply, it is in storage that the actual procedure for multiplication is held. (Often, however, the terms memory and storage are used interchangeably.)

Output. This is the medium through which the computer presents the results of its computations. Output can take several forms. In a hand-held calculator it is the little readout at the top. In a digital watch it is the face of the watch itself. The output device can be a printer that prints the information on paper, thus giving a "hard copy."

Often the input and output are in the same device. For example, the same typewriter that is used to put information into the computer can be used to print out the processed data.

A common type of output is a cathode-ray tube (CRT). In principle the CRT output is very similar to a TV screen. It seems almost natural, therefore, that a TV screen that is used to display the antics of "Charlie's Angels" can also be used to display the output of a computer.

SOFTWARE

The set of instructions that tells a computer what to do is called a *program*. There are two types of programs: systems and applications. The *systems program* tells the computer how to perform certain functions. For example, in

For really big readouts, this operator has connected his personal computer to a 50-inch pro- *jection TV.* GENERAL ELECTRIC *(TV set).*

a calculator the systems program tells the tiny computer how to add, subtract, multiply, find square roots, perform constant functions, and so forth. The *applications program* tells the computer what tasks those functions are to be performed on. If, for example, you write out a mathematical problem with the intent of having the actual computation done by a calculator, what you have written out in effect becomes the applications program.

A TYPICAL PERSONAL COMPUTER

A typical personal computer is likely to consist of the following:

1. A place to store the programs. Usually this will be tape cassettes (the ordinary audio type) and a cassette player. Information is electronically stored on the tape, very similar to the way sound is stored or the way pictures and sound are stored on a videocassette tape.

2. The CPU, which is the actual computing element. Often this is part of the input device contained in the same unit that has the keyboard.

3. Output. In this case the output is your television set. Many small, personal computers come with a screen built into the unit that is used only for that purpose and cannot receive TV programs. In this book we are confining ourselves only to those computers than can be hooked up to your TV screen without disturbing the TV's capabilities of receiving off-the-air and cable broadcasts, and your VCRs and videodiscs.

COMPUTER POWER

A computer's "power", that is, the amount of information it can handle or process, depends on the size of its memory. In computer jargon, units of information are referred to as *bytes*. Computer power is measured in thousands of bytes, represented by the letter K (for *kilo*, which equals 1,000). Thus, a computer with a 48K memory is more powerful than one with a 32K memory. A computer's power can often

be increased by adding on memory that can be purchased separately.

Power can also be increased by using a better memory medium. Somewhat more sophisticated and faster-acting computers use magnetic discs resembling flexible phonograph records instead of cassettes. The major differences between tapes and discs are speed and capacity. To locate a piece of information that has been recorded on tape, the computer must sequentially review *all* the recorded information until it reaches the desired data. Although this process is performed at exceptionally high speed, it is not as fast as the "random access" feature of discs. With *random access memory* (RAM), the computer can randomly select any piece of information that has been recorded and do it instantly. There are a number of personal computers now on the market that have a quantity of RAM as part of the basic system.

Many personal computer systems can accept additional memory by adding on disc drives.
TEXAS INSTRUMENTS, INC.

Furthermore, discs can store much more information than cassettes, which means, first, that the equivalent amount of information takes up less space, and second, that computer systems using discs are likely to perform more because more information is available to them. However, computers with disc memory also usually cost more.

One of the most expensive components of any computer system is the output device. If you have a TV set, then you already own one of the elements that sometimes drives the price of a computer out of reach. Printers can often be the most expensive component of the computer system. They vary in quality and capability, but even the lowest-priced ones cost somewhere around $1,000. With a relatively small additional investment, your video screen can also provide a hard copy. If your need for hard copy is minimal and primarily for your own record-keeping purposes, you could resort to a simple device employed by many computer owners. Use a Polaroid or Kodak camera that can photograph your TV screen

If you don't want to tie up your TV set when using your computer, you can use a TV monitor that serves as the computer's output. This system is displaying an investment portfolio. TEXAS INSTRUMENTS, INC.

and give you an instant picture. (You can, of course, use any other camera if you do not need or want hard copy immediately.)

COMPUTER LANGUAGES

To communicate with a computer it is necessary to use a code which the computer has been instructed to accept. These codes are called *computer languages.* Virtually every personal computer system uses BASIC, an acronym for *B*eginner's *A*ll-purpose *Sy*mbolic *I*nstruction *C*ode. BASIC is about as close to ordinary English as computer languages have come so far. It is relatively simple to learn.

More and more systems and add-ons are being produced in which the instructions given to the computer are also relatively sim-ple, relying on internal electronics to translate the instructions into computer language. With some programs it is only necessary to learn a few basic, elementary instructions to turn the machine on and call up the first part of the program. The screen then displays a set of instructions. When these instructions are followed, the machine programs itself to perform the next phase.

COMPUTER APPLICATIONS

The possible applications of a personal computer are many and varied. The most obvious ones are those of storing and filing information for later recall. If you have a book and record library, if you plan to accumulate a videocassette library, or if you have various collections and files, all of these can be cata-

Many manufacturers supply software packages for use with their computers. This one is *a "command module" for a household budget management system.* TEXAS INSTRUMENTS, INC.

This personal computer system has, in addition to the usual computer features, a built-in music synthesizer. Note game-playing controls at top, which include both key pads and joysticks. APF ELECTRONICS, INC.

logued and cross-referenced on the computer so that instead of rummaging through cassette cases or record stacks while trying to locate a particular rendition of Beethoven's Ninth Symphony, you need only punch the right buttons on your computer and your video screen will then display whatever information you have entered to help you locate the appropriate record. Recipe files, Christmas card mailing lists, records of stocks and bonds—all are fair game for home computers.

In addition, personal computers can help maintain budgets, prepare income tax, update family health and medical records, and can perform myriad other tedious tasks.

I strongly recommend the use of a personal computer and the TV screen to provide for "interactive" video, as opposed to "passive" video. Many educational programs are available for use on personal computer systems. A small sampling includes courses in political science, memory building, basic anatomy, music instruction, foreign languages, geography and history drills, typing, speed reading, and scores of other subjects. Even many video games can be used for instructional purposes. Some, for example, require the solving of mathematical problems in order to win. What is important here is that all such programs require responses from the human participant; the computer will not proceed to the next step until the person operating the system does something.

Of course, many computer programs offer

just plain fun, along with the opportunity to expand creativity. There are programs that allow the operator to compose music, create graphics, and, as mentioned in the previous chapter, create and store one's own games.

Depending on one's needs, it may never be necessary to worry about programming a computer and learning BASIC. An attractive array of software packages is already available to provide a wide variety of functions and instructions. Tax preparation, accounting and inventory systems, and investment portfolios and analyses are just a few of the ready-made programs available to personal computer owners. These software packages cost as little as $15 and as much as $60 for the typical home computer, depending on what they have to do. (There are, of course, some business programs that cost several hundred dollars but are nevertheless a bargain when compared to the cost of an employee to perform the same functions, or the cost of the time that would otherwise have to be spent in performing them.)

One of the most attractive features of virtually every personal computer system is that it can be built up, expanded, and enhanced. For example, you could probably add a *modem* to your home computer. This is a device that enables you, through the use of an ordinary push-button telephone, to link up with data bases virtually anywhere in the world. A *data base* is a kind of library of computerized information. Whatever files or data you store in your own computer is your data base. A major computer installation could be responsible for any number of data bases. An insurance company, for example, could have one data base consisting of actuarial tables, another consisting of all policyholders broken down into categories of policies, and yet a third consisting of names, addresses, and other data concerning every employee who has ever worked for the company. But there are also enormous data bases maintained by private enterprises, various associations, and even government agencies that are accessible through sub-

A modem is a device that enables one computer to "talk" to another over telephone lines.
TEXAS INSTRUMENTS, INC.

scriptions or one-time payment arrangements. For example, the entire New York *Times* data base can be accessed. For $120/hr fee the computer of the New York Times Information Service will take a few key words and search through the files for relevant news stories. The data base includes articles that have appeared in the New York *Times,* the Washington *Post, Time, Newsweek,* and several other publications. Physicians have access to an international network of medical data. Lawyers have similar facilities. There are dozens of data bases currently available on a commercial basis. By the end of the decade there will probably be hundreds that can be easily accessed by anyone with a computer and a telephone.

SHOPPING FOR A PERSONAL COMPUTER

A home computer can cost anywhere from about $300, for a relatively simple unit that uses a cassette recorder and has minimal memory, to a system that incorporates large quantities of memory, disc drives, a hard-copy printer, and costing several thousand dollars. It is difficult to give a price range because the cost of a home computer largely depends on what one buys to go along with it. For example, the Atari 400 Personal Computer System carries a suggested basic retail price of about $650. Depending on what you add on to it, the cost can increase by thousands of dollars. One Atari printer that is compatible with the 400, for example, runs about $500. Another printer, faster and more efficient, sells for double that amount.

When shopping for a computer, here are some factors to take into consideration:

Ease of installation. How does the computer hook up to your TV? There are several methods, the simplest being, as with other video components, hooking up with your TV antenna terminals. Make sure that you understand how the connections are made and that they can be made with relative ease. The signals that a TV set receives are known as *radio frequency* (RF) signals. Most home computers are connected to an *RF modulator* which, in turn, is connected to the antenna terminals. The RF modulator converts the computer's signals to RF signals. Some home computer systems have RF modulators built in, while others have them available as separate accessories. You may have to purchase the RF modulator in addition to the basic computer. They are relatively inexpensive, however. The RF modulator for the Apple II Computer, for example, sells for about $20.

Ease of operation. The instruction and use manuals that come with the home computer are called *documentation.* Carefully check over the documentation for any system before you buy it. Make sure you understand how the machine is operated. You will probably not be able to read through the documentation completely until after you obtain the machine. But at least you should be able to look it over enough to determine whether it is reasonably intelligible. Unfortunately, some computer manufacturers assume a level of sophistication on the part of the user that is not always justified.

Service and maintenance. Computers need tender, loving care. They are complex electronic machines that need occasional service —and that may mean repairs. Many personal computers are constructed with printed circuits; with a little experience the owner can remove a circuit board and replace it with a new one if necessary. Check out the ease of performing repairs in this manner. In addition, check on the availability of qualified service agencies that are readily accessible. It can be something of a nuisance to pack up a computer and ship it back to the factory.

An important benefit that many dealers provide is a free telephone consultation service. Sometimes programs do not run because of a minor bug or hitch in the program itself or the operator's input. Such problems can often be solved over the telephone by a knowledgeable and reputable dealer.

Computer power. The computer's price is mostly determined by its memory. Don't buy a computer more powerful than you need at the moment. On the other hand, don't cut costs by buying a computer that is inadequate for your present needs.

Modularity. Computer systems with add-on capabilities tend to cost more, but in the long run they may prove to be a saving. If you buy a simple system that is totally self-contained and that accepts no accessories or "peripherals" (i.e., units, components, machines, and so forth, that work in conjunction with the computer and give it greater capability), be certain that you will not want to junk the whole thing in six months or a year because of its inadequacy. Similarly, make certain that the peripherals you may want are available, or will be soon, so that you can improve your system when the need or desire to do so arises.

Bear in mind that it is not always necessary to purchase peripherals that are sold by the same company that manufactures the computer. A number of firms supply so-called "plug-compatible" peripherals and devices that easily connect to the computer system of another manufacturer, either directly or through a relatively low-cost and easily attached adaptor.

Software availability. Because of the differences in computer languages and the internal configurations of computer systems, many software packages are not interchangeable except through the performance of some additional programming by the user. Unless you plan to do a great deal of your own programming, be certain that there are a number of software packages available for the system you have in mind. The computer manufacturer's own catalogue of software packages is worth checking into, but it should not be the sole deciding factor. Many independent companies are producing software packages for such popular computers as the Atari Personal Computer System, the Apple, the APF Imagination Machine, the TRS-80 (Radio Shack), Texas Instruments TI099/4 Home Computer, and others.

Hands-on demonstration. If at all possible, try to play with a computer before you buy it. Most cities have computer retail stores. Over the last several years, chains and franchises have sprung up. If you are in or near a large or medium-sized city, chances are there

A developing trend in personal computers involves smaller, lightweight, lower-priced units. This Commodore VIC 20, claimed to be the first full-feature color computer, is priced under $300. COMMODORE INTERNATIONAL, LTD.

is a computer store near you; a quick check in the Yellow Pages will help you locate one.

It is important to get the feel of the machine. It should be comfortable and easy for you to operate. It should also have that nebulous sense of security. Computers are not meant to be abused or beaten up. Nevertheless, the one you buy should feel sturdy and durable.

MAIL-ORDER COMPUTERS

It is possible, should absolute necessity dictate, to purchase a computer, as well as any number of peripherals, by mail order. I would strongly advise against doing so unless you desperately want a computer and there is no other way you can get one. (Such items as tapes or discs, which are not likely to be damaged by excessive handling if properly packed, can generally be ordered by mail without trepidation.) If you must purchase a computer by mail, avoid doing so without taking the following steps:

1. Make sure you thoroughly investigate the unit you want to purchase. Get as much literature as possible from the manufacturer; write or phone to clarify anything you do not understand. Try to familiarize yourself a little with computers generally and the one you have in mind specifically. One way of doing this is to examine some of the computer hobbyists' magazines, which are likely to be available at a well-stocked newsstand and are most certainly available at your local public library.

2. Make sure you are dealing with a reputable supplier. Check out the refund and return policy. Don't hesitate to ask for the names and addresses of other people in your area with whom the firm has done business; then talk to those people.

3. Check on the availability of service and maintenance. Ideally this should be available locally. If that is not possible, determine what problems there may be in having your system repaired, should that ever be necessary.

4. Ask to see a copy of the warranty before you buy.

5. If the mail-order dealer balks at any of the foregoing, find another dealer.

If you know nothing at all about computers, probably the best choice you can make as a beginner is a system that is the best possible unit you can afford, yet one that is fairly basic and simple to operate. It should be a system that can be easily added on to, either with components from the same manufacturer or components made by other companies that are compatible with your system. Then, as your knowledge and interest increase, and as your computer's utility increases, you can gradually upgrade the system.

There is probably no better way to learn about personal computers than through a computer club. They now exist all over the country. If the local Yellow Pages do not readily reveal the names, addresses, and telephone numbers of such clubs, talk to your local librarian. If there is a personal computer retailer in your area, he or she is almost certain to know about existing clubs. If you have settled, more or less, on a particular brand, write to the manufacturer, who will most certainly be able to supply you with the names and addresses of groups of people using their systems.

Members of computer clubs are, understandably, enthusiasts. They know a great deal about computers in general and specific brands in particular. They know what sorts of equipment will perform what sorts of functions and will almost certainly have strong biases, pro and con, toward certain brands. They also know about service and maintenance and can even assist a novice in ironing out the bugs and glitches that are almost certain to appear.

Ted Nelson, writing in *Panorama* magazine (April 1980), has stated that "ultimately, the decision to get a personal computer is like the decision to have a baby—a commitment of time, money, and attention whose justification is, at the last, emotional; it's something you want to care about and become involved with for a long time." For many that is probably true. For others, however, a personal computer is really "a commitment of time, money, and attention" whose justification is, while at least partly emotional, also economic. A computer is, after all, an eminently useful business tool. (Indeed, its purchase price, service, and maintenance costs, as well as the cost of software, may be totally or partially tax deductible, depending on the extent to which it is used for business applications. That is something to check out with your attorney and/or accountant.)

This puts a somewhat different light on the ever-present question: Should you buy now or wait until the technology improves and the prices come down, as is almost certain to happen? Here, at least, you can be a little practical. If you can demonstrate that the acquisition of a small, personal computer will improve your business, maximize efficiency, and earn its price and keep by either reducing costs or increasing revenues, then as a business decision the answer is obvious.

If, however, the "justification is, at the last, emotional," then you need no rational motive. You need only the desire, the money, and the willingness to become intimately involved with a fascinating and versatile piece of machinery.

8

Video Cameras

To find where your true image pictured lies . . .

—*Sonnets,* XXIV

The temptation to produce one's own video programs is almost irresistible, especially for those who have a penchant for making home movies. There are, in fact, a number of parallels. For one thing, an amateur home movie can be anything, from a collection of disjointed, boring, and generally badly made pictures of little meaning or interest to anyone other than the maker and the subjects to a sophisticated, near-professional production. All of the reasons for making home movies apply to home video programs: record-keeping; information and instruction; and an outlet for creative urges.

There are certain advantages and disadvantages to both videotape and conventional movie film. For one thing, videotape is considerably cheaper. One hour of filming with a conventional super-8mm camera would consume approximately twenty rolls of film at a total cost of about $160. (Moreover, you may wind up with a silent movie.) A videotape, however, can record both sound and picture for about $15 and provide up to six hours of viewing time. Furthermore, the results of the videotape effort are instantaneous. It is not necessary to deliver a videocassette to the corner drugstore, a drive-in booth, or a letter box for mailing to a processing company. Further economy derives from the fact that the tape can be used over and over again—up to a point. (After thirty or forty reuses it begins to wear out.) With conventional film, once you've shot it you've got it.

Film, however, does offer certain advantages over tape. It is likely to be much more

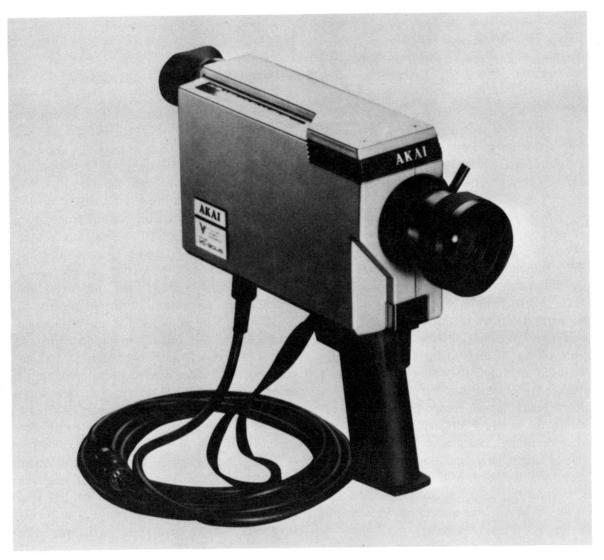

A color video camera with a zoom lens, through-the-lens viewfinder, and built-in condenser microphone. Focusing is done with a *split-image rangefinder superimposed on the viewfinder.* AKAI AMERICA, LTD.

durable. The initial cost of the equipment is considerably less. And, finally, film offers greater portability. As discussed in Chapter 4, several companies are now producing VCRs that are extremely lightweight and can be hooked up to your camera. The cameras themselves, as we shall soon see, are also extremely light. Nevertheless, an amateur movie camera, equipped with a microphone, that has

the capability of recording picture and sound (on a magnetic stripe running alongside the film) is smaller and lighter than any portable VCR-camera combination.

This points up the major difference between a movie camera and a video camera. In a movie camera the storage medium—the film —is located right inside the camera. Thus, the camera in effect stores what it records. With a video camera the picture must be transmitted to the recording medium—videotape. According to a recent *Consumer Reports,* a portable VCR and color camera combination costs about $2,400; for black and white the cost is about $1,600. This compares with about $1,000 for a camera, a projector, and screen for making and showing super-8mm sound movies. *Consumer Reports* points out, however, that "for the price of two reels of super-8 color sound film—running time six minutes and forty seconds—you can buy a videocassette that provides at least two hours of recording time."

While we are on the subject of costs, it should be emphasized that this chapter deals only with video cameras for home video systems. Obviously, as is true for most of the equipment described in this book, video cameras range from small, lightweight, and fairly simple affairs to highly complex, heavy-duty TV-studio equipment costing thousands of dollars. Also, while the basic principles of camera function and components remain essentially the same for all cameras, commercial and professional equipment has achieved a level of complexity and sophistication that goes beyond the scope of this book. If they are not beyond the scope of your interest, then you should be thinking about commercial television rather than home video.

Home video cameras represent a dramatic example of improving technology versus lower costs. Initially color cameras were so expensive that most amateurs and hobbyists confined themselves to black-and-white units. In the early 1970s a color camera could cost as much as $10,000. Within a decade a basic color camera for the hobbyist could be purchased for under $700. Black-and-white cameras can now be purchased for as little as $200 to $250. These prices are for basic models. The more deluxe versions start at about $500 for black and white and $1,000 for color. A deluxe model camera offers a variety of features, many of which are automatic or electronically controlled, that, as with still

and motion-picture film cameras, generally provide for easier and more convenient operation.

THE BASIC VIDEO CAMERA

The basic components of a TV camera are the lens, the vidicon tube, the viewfinder, and the "video out."

As with any camera, light is reflected off the subject and passes through the lens. In a TV camera the light strikes a tube called a *vidicon.* The vidicon tube converts light signals to electrical signals while at the same time adjusting the contrast and brightness. The signal is then sent to the video-out receptacle at the back of the camera, into which is connected the recording device—typically a VCR. (A TV monitor or TV set can also be connected to the camera to produce instant home TV shows that are not recorded. In general, we will be discussing the making of recordings on tape. However, you may want to occasionally indulge in "instant video" as a kind of dry run or dress rehearsal—or just for the fun of it.)

Lens. How much a lens "sees" is determined by its focal length. The focal length is the distance between the center of the lens and the point at which the image is in focus. In a film camera that point is the plane in which the film is situated. In a video camera that point is the *target plate* of the vidicon tube. The focal length is described in millimeters (mm).

The size of the lens is an indication of how much the lens will take in. In video cameras a 25-mm lens provides an average or medium field of view, a 50-mm lens brings the subject in closer, and a 12.5-mm lens moves the image farther back, offering a wide angle of view. The shorter the focal length (i.e., the lower the number), the wider the angle of view. The longer the focal length, the closer in it brings the subject.

Thus, a camera with a fixed-focus lens offers a fixed field of view. To alter the per-

This deluxe camera includes, as standard equipment, an automatic iris, zoom lens, low-light capability, electronic viewfinder, and a number of other features. According to the manufacturer, it is the first camera to offer automatic continuous focusing. TOSHIBA AMERICA, INC.

spective, either the subject or the camera must be moved. Another way of altering the perspective is to remove the lens and replace it with one having another focal length. Depending, of course, upon the subject and the circumstances, such changes can be no problem at all—or they can be extremely awkward.

Zoom lens. A zoom lens is one that has a variable focal length. By operating the proper control, you can move closer to or farther away from the subject without physically moving the camera or the subject. The zoom control may consist of a ring which is either rotated or pushed back and forth along the length of the lens housing. Some units come equipped with a lever for ease of operation. Others are equipped with an electronic power zoom which, at the push of a button, slides the lens back and forth until the desired image is achieved.

It is my personal opinion that a zoom lens is an object greatly to be desired. It provides for an infinite number of focal lengths at any point between its farthest and nearest limits. If you are photographing someone standing under an apple tree, you could begin with a picture of the entire scene and then, with a single sweeping motion of the lens's control, gradually zoom in for a close-up of the subject's face. You could also stop anywhere along the way for the desired image. A zoom lens permits the operator to compose images in the viewfinder with a most satisfying degree of accuracy.

Focus. The focus control adjusts the lens so that the maximum amount of sharpness is achieved—or, if you prefer, a degree of fuzziness which works surprisingly well for creating certain special effects.

Iris. This control determines the amount of light entering the lens. Generally, once the iris is set for a pleasing result, it is left alone for the rest of the sequence unless the lighting changes dramatically. The iris is also referred to as the *diaphragm,* the terms being used interchangeably. Some video cameras are equipped with automatic diaphragms that adjust the opening in accordance with the lighting conditions.

Most of the automatic features on a video camera, such as an automatic iris and power zoom, can also be operated manually when necessary and/or desirable.

Color temperature. Although the human optical system is capable of adjusting to differences in various types of light sources, mechanical and electronic optical systems usually are not. Different light sources have different color components. Most video cameras are balanced for daylight. Other light sources, however, can result in pictures with an overall greenish, bluish, yellowish, or reddish cast. This is described as the light's *color temperature* and is measured in *degrees Kelvin* (°K), so named for the scientist who developed the measurement system. Some of the more basic video cameras require the correction or adjustment of color temperatures by the placement of an optical filter over the front of the lens. Most, however, are equipped with a control to adjust for color temperature. Frequently this simply consists of a dial with a pointer that is moved to an appropriate little picture indicating the type of light source. The adjustments are usually made by a unit known as the *color control unit* (CCU). With most cameras the CCU is built into the circuitry. It is possible to obtain an external CCU which allows for considerable fine-tuning of the color. However, this involves the purchase of another piece of equipment, one which has to be carried around when shooting on location. Unless you are planning exceptionally high-quality productions approximating professional programs, it is probably best to avoid cameras requiring an external CCU.

White balance control. Closely related to the notion of varying color temperatures is the fact that while something may look white to you, it could appear reddish or bluish to the camera. Cameras that have a white balance control enable you to focus on a white object and then adjust for excessive blue or red (in accordance with the instructions in the camera's operating manual) until the proper balance is achieved. Once the white balance control has been set, most of the other colors will also be brought into proper balance.

Optical viewfinder. It is virtually impossible to have any accurate idea of what your camera is seeing without a viewfinder. An optical viewfinder is constructed a little like a telescope that has been mounted backward. It sits at the top of the camera and allows you to see, more or less, what the camera is looking at.

A version of the optical viewfinder is the *through-the-lens* (TTL) type, which functions like the viewfinder on a 35-mm single-lens reflex camera. The TTL viewfinder enables you to see exactly what the lens sees. It eliminates some of the guesswork necessary with an ordinary optical viewfinder, since the optical finder will not show you whether you are in focus or whether you have set the iris at the correct opening for the prevailing light conditions. (With optical viewfinders some guess-work will most certainly be involved, although it will surely improve with experience. A light meter may help.)

Electronic viewfinder. If you cannot afford to buy a camera that is already equipped with an electronic viewfinder, try to get one that will accept such a viewfinder as an add-on accessory later. The electronic viewfinder looks like a tiny TV screen through which a minuscule portion of the video signal is transmitted prior to passing through the video-out socket.

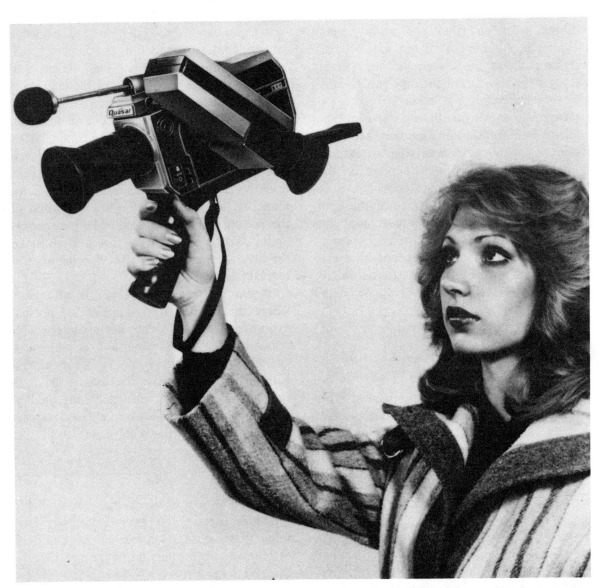

With an adjustable-mount electronic view-finder it is possible to aim the camera over the heads of crowds or create unusual angles. As long as you can see through the viewfinder, you can see what is being recorded. Note the built-in boom microphone. QUASAR CO.

It enables you to see exactly what the camera sees and exactly what will be recorded.

Most electronic viewfinders give a little more, too. Along the edges of the viewfinder's picture there are various indicators supplying such information as the adequacy of the power supply and whether the image is under- or over-exposed. Another rather nice advantage of the electronic viewfinder is the fact that it can serve as a tiny viewing screen when the recording tape is played back. It is an excellent way to make certain that everything is in proper working order and that you are recording the picture you want. It is not unlike beginning an audio taping session and then playing back a short segment of the tape just to make sure that the recording is "taking."

Microphone. All but the most basic video cameras have built-in microphones. Most also have the capability of accepting an external microphone. In general, most experts feel that the built-in microphones are adequate, nothing more. If the resonant tones of the company glee club or the mellifluous mouthings of the local drama society are an important aspect of what you plan to record, you may want to consider the use of an external microphone. (These are discussed in greater detail in the next chapter.)

OTHER FEATURES

It bears repeating that, as with most other video equipment, the initial purchase price of a video camera depends almost entirely on the features and conveniences built into it. This price covers the basics—camera body, lens, vidicon tube, video-out receptacle, and some sort of viewfinder—after which you are paying for additions and refinements.

Whatever those additions and refinements may be, it is essential to make sure that they are compatible with your VCR. When purchasing a camera, discuss your VCR with the dealer. For one thing, if you do not already own a VCR, you may want to purchase a system, that is, a camera and VCR that were essentially made for each other. If you already own a VCR, however, it may be necessary to also acquire special adaptors to connect the camera you have in mind to your VCR. For the most part, such adaptors are usually low-priced, but it is a good idea to check on their availability and ease of application.

If you have a VCR that is compatible, you may want a camera that comes equipped with a switch that permits you to turn the VCR on or off and set the recorder on "pause" while you are holding or operating the camera.

Another nice touch that will almost certainly add to the overall cost of the camera is automatic fade. This is a control that electronically provides for fading out of or into a scene. (Fades will be discussed in Chapter 10.)

Many cameras also include a backlight control. If your subject is standing in front of a brightly illuminated background, the automatic iris will adjust for the bright portion of the picture and the subject will be under-exposed. With a backlight control you can make the necessary adjustments for special or dramatic effects.

If you expect to be taping in situations where the lighting is insufficient for normal exposure, you should consider a camera with a low-light feature. This permits the camera to "gain" more light (the control is often called a gain switch). Typically, the use of the gain switch causes some sacrifice in picture quality. In many instances, however, a less-than-perfect picture is better than no picture at all.

ACCESSORIES

A wide variety of accessories are available for video cameras. In general, virtually anything that can fit over the lens of a still or movie camera to alter the image can also be used over the lens of a video camera. There are special filters, for example, that can adjust for color temperature. (Some video cameras have such filters built in.) These filters can also be used for dramatic special effects. Colored filters can give an overall coloration to the scene. Certain optical filters can turn pinpoints of light into "cross stars." There are others that provide soft focus for a kind of ethereal effect. Still others transmit multiple images of the same subject.

If you already own a still or motion picture camera with interchangeable lenses, you should investigate the possibility of using some or all of those lenses on a video camera. Often a simple and inexpensive adaptor will enable you to switch a lens from a film camera to a video camera.

If you do not already own a tripod, you should probably buy one when you purchase a video camera. It has a number of worthwhile uses. One of its chief advantages, surprisingly, is that it permits greater mobility when setting up a scene. Imagine getting everything just right: Your zoom lens is at exactly the right focal length; the scene in your viewfinder is framed precisely the way you want it; and the iris has been adjusted properly for the light. You are ready to shoot, when you notice that one of the props is a little out of place, someone is not standing exactly right, or clothing needs adjustment. With your camera on a tripod (assuming you have mounted it firmly and properly), you can leave the camera and walk over to the scene to make the necessary adjustments. Otherwise you will either have to set the camera down on the floor or carry it with you, which means you will have to set the scene up in the viewfinder all over again.

The most important use of a tripod, however, has to do with camera movement. It is now possible to purchase a video camera that weighs as little as four pounds. Inevitably, some degree of art has to be sacrificed on behalf of weight. A lightweight camera moves much more easily and is more responsive to slight shakes and tremors. Camera movement is even more exaggerated when telephoto lenses are being used or when a zoom lens brings the subject exceptionally close. A tripod is an excellent device for greatly minimizing unwanted camera movement.

CAMERA CARE

The vidicon tube is a delicate and sensitive object that requires gentle handling. In addition, lenses and the other components of a video camera can be knocked out of alignment and even seriously damaged by rough handling. A general attitude of respect toward one's equipment is likely to be repaid by long and efficient service. When it comes to cameras, the following few specifics should be attended to:

1. When the camera is not in use, keep the lens covered. This will protect the lens and will also avoid the accidental exposure of the vidicon tube to bright lights.

2. After you have covered the lens, make sure that the camera has been turned off. Otherwise the vidicon tube will wear itself out trying to record and convert the near-total blackness created by the lens cap.

3. Always avoid directing the camera at subjects of extremely high contrast for any extended length of time. Otherwise the image may "burn in" on the vidicon tube and will then show up on all subsequent scenes as a ghostly reminder of improper handling.

4. Similarly, extremely bright objects, including highly reflective metal objects and the sun itself, can permanently damage the vidicon tube and should be avoided. (One advantage of an automatic iris is that it prevents an accidental burn on the camera tube.)

5. Never drop the camera.

6. Read Chapter 9.

WHICH CAMERA TO BUY?

As with every other component of a home video system that we discussed, price, of course, is a major determining factor. The type of camera you buy will be limited by

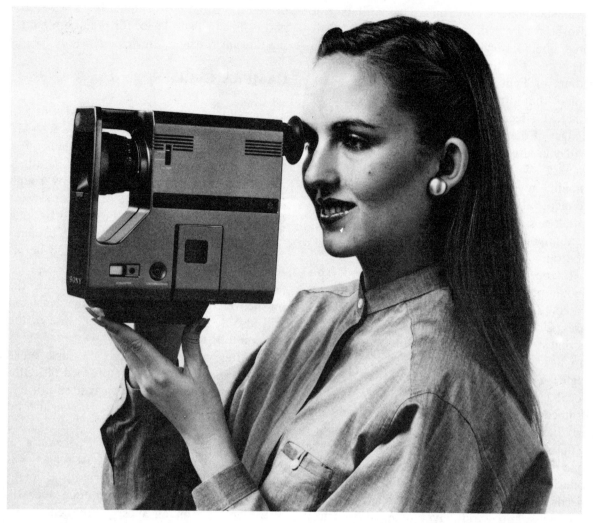

In July 1980 Sony showed this prototype of a portable video camera that contains video- tape for recording the image. Production is promised for 1985. A few months later Hitachi *also introduced a single-unit camera, promised for 1982 or 1983. Both use ultra small cas- settes.* SONY CORP. OF AMERICA.

the amount of money you are willing to spend. But perhaps more than with any other com- ponent, personal temperament and proclivi- ties enter into the decision about obtaining a video camera. The question is not only how much you can afford but how much gadgetry you want.

The most basic black-and-white video cam- era will perform the most basic functions and fulfill a wide variety of basic needs. It is cer- tainly adequate, for example, for creating a visual record of your valuables for insurance purposes or for recording such events as your child's first birthday or someone's first wed- ding. It is not adequate for creating very many special effects and producing a "film" that approaches some degree of professionalism. But that may not be what you need or want.

If you simply prefer to point and shoot, something like a zoom lens can be more of a hindrance than a help. Personal attitudes toward home video cameras are the same as those toward film cameras. If you should ever find yourself peering into the Grand Canyon or leaning on the rail of the Statue of Liberty ferryboat, observe the other tourists who are happily clicking away. Some have expensive cameras with all sorts of attachments that either require meticulous adjustment or are equipped with electronic automatic devices. Many others, however, are perfectly happy with their point-and-shoot Instamatics. Who is to say that one is better than the other?

If you are uncertain as to your own preferences and desires, then caution and conservatism are the order of the day. Look for a camera that gives you what you need and want now but that will also accept bigger and better "bells and whistles" (a popular phrase among both camera and video buffs for the little extras). A video camera can and should grow with its user.

9

Maintaining a Home Video System

Have a care of your entertainments . . .

—*The Merry Wives of Windsor*, IV, v

This chapter is concerned with such matters as maintenance, repairs, and accessories—both great and small—that could prove useful, or at least amusing. Although it has been stated before, it seems particularly appropriate here to restate the by now familiar caveat: This is a book about *home* video and everything in it relates to home video. Perhaps in no other chapter could one extend one's interests—and purchases—well beyond the limits of the home as much as in this one.

There are accessories, equipment, appliances, and appurtenances for video the mere listing of which could easily fill a book twice this size. It would be wasteful and excessive, however, to discuss at length such objects as,

for example, camera dollies, those rubber-tired trucks that TV studios use for moving about cameras and camera operators. Or the earphones and microphones that TV directors use to communicate with camera operators. Or expensive and elaborate lighting equipment. Or camera switchers that enable the switching of the image being broadcast from one camera to another. Or all of the various kinds of electronic devices for enhancing video and audio recording and reproduction. Or all the sophisticated editing equipment.

As is true of almost any hobby or pastime, some amateurs have equipment and facilities that any professional would be glad to use. There is, of course, nothing to prevent you from converting your basement to a fully equipped TV studio—nothing but inclination, finances, and the tolerance level of other members of your family. If you want to do that, however, you will have to resort to more professional and technical literature.

There is yet another genre of home video user whose existence I acknowledge but whose proclivities I cannot accommodate: the gadget lover. There are among us individuals who are technology freaks. It really does not matter what the end result of the use of a particular piece of equipment or device might be; technology freaks are perfectly happy merely using the gimmicks. (I have a friend whose technological freakiness inevitably led him into the field of photography. I used to describe his passion by saying that if he could figure out some way of using the equipment without having to bother taking pictures, he would be the happiest man in the world. He has since discovered that personal computers and all their ramifications are far more satisfying than photographic gadgetry. He is a truly happy man.)

Let us assume, therefore, that your interest is in owning and using a home video system that can add pleasure and instruction to your life—rather than one that will take over your life—and proceed accordingly.

IN THE BEGINNING . . .

There is probably no better way to accidentally damage a piece of video equipment, possibly beyond repair, than to attempt to operate it without first reading the accompanying instruction manual. By taking a little extra time, you can save considerably more time, not to mention aggravation and expense. Furthermore, you will probably ultimately derive greater pleasure and use from the equipment. The procedure is simple.

First, without going anywhere near the equipment, read the instruction manual through from beginning to end. Make sure you understand everything. If you do not, call

or visit the dealer and ask for an explanation. (Ideally, you should try to read the instruction manual—or at least those parts of it that deal with basic operation—in the store before you buy.)

After you have read through the manual, start all over again on page 1, this time with the equipment close at hand. The equipment should not be connected to anything, including the electricity. Identify and operate all of the parts exactly as instructed in the manual.

Once you feel confident that you know where everything is and how it should work, plug the thing in and start all over again on page 1. Be sure to check that everything is working as it is supposed to, especially those features for which you may not have an immediate need. If you decide to use one of those features for the first time after the warranty has expired and only then discover that it is not functioning properly, you will be out of luck. The defect may have been in the unit from the start, but you will still have to pay to have it corrected.

GENERAL CARE

Most manufacturers make a genuine effort to build their equipment as sturdily as design, technology, and costs will permit. They also try to achieve as much simplicity of operation as possible. Nevertheless, these units consist of intricate and delicate electronic mechanisms, many of which are critically balanced and aligned. Two general rules, therefore, should be meticulously observed:

1. Be clean.
2. Be gentle.

When your equipment is not being used, it should be covered. Bits of tobacco, ash, food particles, and moisture can all do serious damage to most video equipment. It is best, therefore, to avoid eating, drinking, or smoking while using any of the components. (Probably for reasons of discretion, none of the manuals or advice-givers deal with the one remaining vice. There are apparently no direct harmful effects on video equipment caused by sex. In fact, some owners of home video systems have been known to find various creative ways of employing those systems during sex. Should you be similarly inclined, you need only remember that eating, drinking, smoking, and moisture in general are not good for the video equipment. If the equipment is kept well away from the scene of the action, nothing amiss should occur—at least to the video equipment.)

Avoid using any equipment that has been subjected to temperature extremes. You may be anxious to demonstrate the latest cassette you just purchased to the rest of the family. If you are coming in from the cold, you should allow the cassette to warm up to room temperature. You should also allow your equipment to warm up for a minute or so before using it. Temperature changes can cause condensation, stiffness, and a reduction in the power supply. A little patience will go a long way toward efficient operation.

Even if your equipment has the kind of electronic switching that permits immediate transference from one mode to another, it is best not to traumatize the machinery. Pause for a second or two between modes or functions. The sudden transition from one mode to another can cause the unit to stop or start unevenly, which not only puts unnecessary stress on the moving parts but can cause such problems as cinching, a kind of bunching or wrinkling of the tape that can become permanent if left unattended. (To correct cinching, rewind the tape to one end and then allow it to wind fully to the other end without interruption. If cinching continues to occur, there is probably a problem with your VCR which should be attended to professionally.)

CLEANING AND MAINTENANCE

It may seem silly to go into a store to purchase a can of air, but that can of air can be one of the most useful tools in your maintenance kit. Almost all photo supply shops sell little cans of compressed air with long plastic tubes attached. They are excellent for cleaning dust and loose dirt from cameras, lenses, tubes, VCRs, and other components with areas that are either too difficult to reach or too delicate to touch.

Another useful accessory obtainable from camera stores is a high-quality brush, such as one made of camel's-hair. If you cannot buy a good brush, do not buy any. A cheap brush will only cause aggravation by indiscriminately dropping hairs where you neither want nor need them. Some camera stores can supply brushes that are attached to little rubberlike blowers so that you can brush off the dirt and dust and administer a small, gentle puff of air at the same time.

Tape heads. As tape continues to be used and reused, either for recording new material over old or for continuous playback, some of the tiny magnetized particles may wear off, resulting in "drop-out." You know this is happening when portions of the picture are replaced by small areas of black or white, which means that parts of the picture have "dropped out." As the tape passes through the tape heads of the VCR, constant pressure and friction cause wear on the surface of the tape. Similarly, the loose particles cause wear on the heads. It is essential, therefore, to keep the tape heads clean so as to reduce the wear both on the heads and on the tapes.

A videocassette recorder contains four sets of heads: one for recording and playing back the video portion of the program, another for the audio portion, a third, called "control track heads," which, as the name implies, are concerned with those tracks on the tape that contain the pulses that control the tape's speed, and the erase heads. Each of these sets of heads can become dirty with use, primarily from oxides deposited by the tape. It is easy to tell when the heads need cleaning: Invariably an appreciable and annoying loss in both sound and picture quality becomes evident.

Unless you are extremely adept mechanically and/or enjoy taking risks, *leave the heads in the VCR alone.* The instant you touch your screwdriver to the VCR, you void the warranty. What is worse, in attempting to take the thing apart, you could do even more damage, resulting in repair costs far greater than it would have cost to simply replace heads that may have been irreparably worn out. If you absolutely insist on getting inside the machine yourself, there are video-head cleaning kits that are designed specifically for home VCRs. Your dealer, or such electrical supply companies as Radio Shack and Lafayette Radio, should be able to supply them.

The best way for a cautious novice to clean his VCR heads at home is to purchase a cleaning cassette that fits the machine. A number of major cassette manufacturers supply them. You simply run the cleaning cassette through the machine for the indicated time, which could range anywhere from ten to thirty seconds, and then see the results. If you still think the heads are not functioning properly, it is best to seek professional help.

After some considerable use, the heads in a VCR may become magnetized. This could result in poor or noisy audio, poor picture quality, picture distortion, or even blank spots on the picture, indicating that the tape is being partially erased. Even if none of these symptoms appears, it is probably a good idea to demagnetize the VCR head at every fifth or sixth cleaning.

A device called a *head demagnetizer* (sometimes also called a degausser) is required. If you already have such a device for your audio equipment, you can use it on your

This video-head cleaning kit includes special chamois-type applicators and a bottle of cleaning formula. The items are also available individually. ROBINS INDUSTRIES CORP.

Most major tape manufacturers supply video-head cleaning cassettes in both the VHS and Beta formats. FUJI PHOTO FILM USA, INC., MAGNETIC TAPE DIV.

VCR. However, if you do have such a device, then you also know that it requires considerable skill to manipulate it. To function properly the demagnetizer must be placed extremely close to the head. However, the demagnetizer vibrates at a very high speed. If it touches the head, its vibrations can cause damage. As a simple precaution, cover the tip of the demagnetizer with electrician's tape; then, if the demagnetizer touches the head, no damage will be done.

To demagnetize the heads, first turn off the VCR and remove any cassettes. (The unit will also demagnetize tapes. Demagnetizing tapes is the same as erasing them.) Switch on the demagnetizer and place the probe as close as possible, first to the video heads, then the erase heads, the control heads, and the audio heads. Then slowly pass the demagnetizer along the tape path to remove any magnetic charge which the metal guides may have accumulated. *Slowly* move the demagnetizer several feet from the unit before switching it off. The reason for the slow removal relates to the fact that while this device is called a demagnetizer, it is, in fact, a magnetizer. It functions by magnetizing the heads first in one direction and then in another; in effect, the second magnetization cancels out the first, and so on. By turning the unit off while it is still close to the heads, you may fail to allow for the full cancelling-out process.

Lubrication. The most important rule to remember here is that if you do not know, do not guess. Follow the manufacturer's instructions to the letter. Chances are that a small quantity of lubricating oil will be packed right in with the equipment. If it is not, use a very light machine oil. Check with your dealer or an electronics supply store for the best kind.

Some well-intentioned but misinformed would-be mechanics are under the impression that if a little oil helps something work smoothly, a lot of oil should help it run perfectly. Nothing could be further from the truth. On the contrary, excess oil can be devastating. A tiny quantity can virtually ruin a videotape. That is why there should be no tape in the unit while you are doing the lubricating. Even so, if you use too much oil, the excess will spill onto the tape that you put in after you are finished. Oil that drips where it does not belong can also damage circuits and connections and interfere with their proper functioning. Equally serious is the fact that even small puddles of unwanted oil attract dust and dirt.

REPAIRING VIDEOTAPES

There comes a time in the life of every user of recording tape, whether audio or video, when the tape misbehaves. For any number of reasons a tape can jam in a machine. Sometimes the fault lies in the mechanics of the cassette itself. A cheap cassette has cheap works. An old cassette has worn out works. Sudden and erratic stops and starts, resulting either from haphazard and careless operation of the equipment or because of some flaw or defect in the mechanics of the equipment itself, can cause tape to snap, loop, and wind itself around one of the moving parts. When that happens, never attempt to rip the tape out. Most tapes are made of Mylar or some similar extremely tough and resilient material that resists tearing. As you rip out the tape, you are likely to rip out a small piece of the machinery along with it. Try—gently, carefully, and slowly—to unwind the tape by grasping it and pushing it back in the general direction from which it came. This probably will not work, but it is worth a try. Alternately, take a small, sharp pair of scissors and very carefully cut away the tape that has gotten jammed inside the machine. Be very careful to keep the two ends that have been cut free well out of the cassette. Pull them out a few inches if necessary. Then use a pair of tweezers to very gently extract the remaining bits of tape that are still in the machine.

It may be possible to rescue the tape still in

the cassette. It requires the patience, care, and skill of a surgeon. What you must do is open the cassette, find and splice the ends of the tape, and then close the cassette again—all without disturbing the configuration of the tape within. If you have the courage and the fortitude to try, this is the procedure to follow:

1. Turn the cassette over and use a small Phillips-type screwdriver to remove the retaining screws.

2. Very carefully turn the cassette over again, with the label facing you, making sure that the cassette does not come apart as you turn it.

3. At the left side of the cassette you will find the front-panel release catch. Press it down and open the tape protector panel.

4. The tape protector panel is spring-loaded. While holding it with one hand, remove the cover of the cassette.

5. Cut away the unwanted tape. Then overlap the ends of the good tape and cut through them at a right angle. Carefully align the ends of the tape and splice with video splicing tape. Be very careful to avoid twisting one or the other of the ends of the tape. The splicing tape should be placed on the back, or shiny side, of the videotape. (The dull side is the recording surface.)

6. Carefully rewind the tape manually into the cassette, making sure that it passes through its tape guides.

7. Reassemble the cassette by following steps 1 through 4 in reverse order.

8. Pray.

CAMERA CARE

Accumulations of dust and fingerprints on camera lenses should be removed as soon as possible. Do not, however, use facial tissues or those little tissues sold in drugstores that are intended for cleaning eyeglasses. Almost all lenses are coated with special materials that are highly sensitive to the abrasive properties of these products. Use a special lens cleaning tissue or, where necessary, a lens cleaning fluid. Both are available at photo-supply shops. The fluid should be applied with a cotton swab (such as Q-tips) or a lintless cloth. Excess fluid should also be removed with a dry cotton swab or a lintless cloth.

If spots and smudges appear on your picture and cleaning the lens does not eliminate them, it may be necessary to clean the vidicon tube. The first rule is *always be very careful.* The lens should be gently and carefully removed in accordance with the camera's instruction manual. Then, using the lens cleaning fluid and a cotton swab, carefully and gently clean the surface of the camera tube, which will probably be visible when the lens is removed. Move the camera around so that you can see the entire surface of the tube, cleaning where necessary. Replace the lens and then turn on the camera and either the TV set or the VCR. Check the picture to see if the spots and smudges still appear. If they do, try cleaning the tube again. If you are certain that you have cleaned the lens and the tube thoroughly, then those spots and smudges may be burned in on the tube, in which case the tube needs to be replaced.

CLEANING CABINETS, CASINGS, AND HOUSINGS

A manufacturer who does not include in the instructions information on how to clean the outer shell of the unit is, at best, remiss. In general, manufacturers' instructions should be followed. Where there are none, use a very mild detergent and lukewarm water. (This applies, of course, to plastic and metal; water and detergent should not be used on wood or on any other surface when specifically prohibited in the instruction manual.)

I have found that the little napkinlike sheets, such as Wash 'n Dri, impregnated with a mild cleanser consisting primarily of alcohol are excellent for taking along on field trips. They are not only good for refreshing oneself, as advertised, but are very useful on metal and plastic housings. They do a reasonably good cleaning job, are fairly mild (because they are made to be used on human skin), and the moisture that they apply to a surface evaporates very quickly. (Do *not* use them on lenses.)

If a cabinet or casing becomes really grubby or encrusted, or if it is defiled by some particularly vile and unusual substance, it is probably better to use frequent applications of a mild soap or detergent and water than to attempt to remove the filthy stuff with some strong solvent that will probably clean the surface but will also damage it and perhaps even dissolve some plastic materials. It is best to tolerate the dirt for a little while until you can call or write the manufacturer for instructions.

CABLES AND CONNECTORS

Home video systems can work only if all the connections are properly made. Therefore, if something is not working, the first things to check are the connections and hookups. In order to function properly, cables, plugs, sockets, and connectors require a reasonable amount of care. For the best possible service from the various connectors and cables, you would do to well to refer occasionally to the following basic checklist:

1. Begin with quality products. Get the best you can afford. Avoid bargains, closeouts, and off brands unless you're enough of an expert to know exactly what you're getting. Cables and connectors are not always inexpensive, but cutting corners can often mean false economy, because a poorly made connector can result in a poor production or, even worse, serious damage to your equipment.

2. If your video system becomes complicated and sophisticated, life will become much easier if you devise some suitable technique for keeping track of what gets hooked up where. Here are several possible methods:

A. Keep a log, journal, or diary of how various connections are to made.

B. Use little stickers with matching numbers to show what gets plugged in where. You could, for example, label all plugs with an A series, such as A-1, A-2, A-3, and so forth, and label the corresponding receptacles with a B series. Thus, it will be easy to remember that plug A-4 is to be inserted into receptacle B-4.

C. A variation on this theme is a color code using bits of colored tape to mark the cables, plugs, connectors, and receptacles.

D. Draw a diagram or chart that shows the various connections.

3. Never force anything. If a connection cannot be made easily, you are either attempting to hook up the wrong components or you have something in an improper position. If you try to force a hookup, you are almost certain to break something.

4. Dirt interferes seriously with proper connections. Keep all cables and wires free of dirt and dust. All connectors should be cleaned periodically. (Make sure, however, that everything is unplugged when you do so, or you may never again have to worry about whether anything at all is working.)

5. Keep all wires, plugs, switches, cables, and equipment away from curious children and/or pets. Such creatures can do serious damage to themselves, not to mention the equipment.

6. Treat cables and connectors with care. Do not allow connector ends to drop onto the floor or to remain there, where they can be stepped on. Cables should not be bent, tied, or twisted. For storage and transport, it is best to wind cables into coils of about 15 inches in diameter.

Most of the connectors, plugs, and other similar parts you use can probably be replaced fairly readily at a video dealer or at an electronic-supply store. There are also a number of mail-order houses that supply such items. If you are making your purchase in person, take

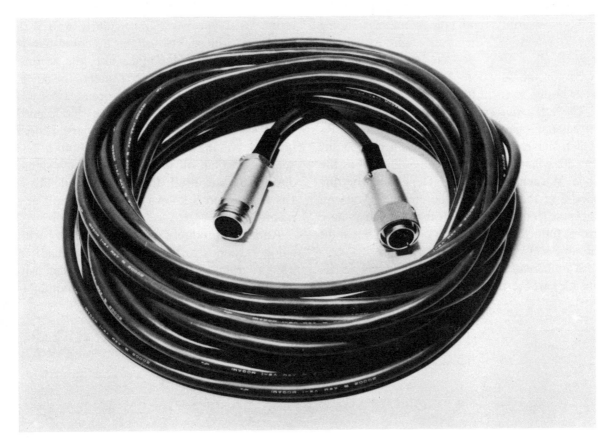

Cables for connecting components should be stored or carried in loose coils. Connectors *should be protected from dirt and damage.* TOTAL VIDEO SUPPLY CO.

the damaged or worn part with you; this is the easiest way for the salesperson to identify and replace it. If you are ordering by mail, give the part number or any other specific identification.

On occasion a salesperson will offer you a part that looks a little different and carries a different number because it is made by another manufacturer. He or she may tell you that it is better, cheaper, or the only thing in stock. Unless you have reason to doubt this, take the salesperson's word for it—up to a point. As soon as you get the new part home, try it out. Don't wait until you need it to discover that this individual made a mistake.

When you purchase something new for your system, have with you the brand name and model number of the unit for which the accessory is being purchased. If the unit is small, such as a video camera or a portable VCR, take it along with you for an on-the-spot fitting. This applies not only to cables and connectors, of course, but to all of the accessories which we will discuss.

ACCESSORIES AND ADD-ONS

Here, for your delectation and curiosity, are offered a number of accessories, almost all of which you can probably do very well without.

They are designed to increase or enhance the utility, versatility, and enjoyment of a home video system. Whether you ought to acquire any or all of them depends entirely on your need for the functions they perform and on your ability to resist temptation.

Cassette changers. There are several models of cassette changers available for Beta VCRs which make it possible to stack a number of cassettes that are automatically changed as the tape in each is depleted. Depending on the model of the VCR and the changer, you can increase continuous recording time anywhere from four to twenty hours. Prices begin at about $100.

Commercial eliminators. This is a wonderful idea whose time has come but whose technology is somewhat lacking. There are several types. One type works particularly well with black-and-white movies. Even though a film is being telecast in black and white, the accompanying commercials are usually in color. This unit senses the color broadcasts and switches the VCR into the "pause" mode until the black-and-white picture reappears. Unfortunately, if the engineer at the studio has neglected to cut off the color broadcast signal during the film itself, the "commercial killer" (as this device is known) will not permit any recording.

Another product, one that works with color, responds to the fade technique used in TV programs. Typically, the TV screen will fade to black immediately before a commer-

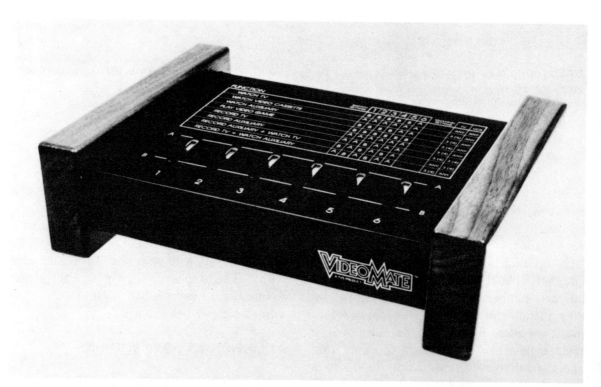

This switcher is capable of accepting connections for a VCR, a videodisc player, antenna or cable, video game, home computer, and satellite or cable converter. TOTAL VIDEO SUPPLY CO.

cial. This unit senses the fade and switches the VCR to the "pause" mode. During the following 60 seconds it keeps searching for another fade. If it finds one, it will resume the pause-and-search cycle. If, after 30 seconds, no other fade occurs, it will release the "pause" control and resume recording. Unfortunately, the screen also fades to black *after* the commercial is over and the program resumes, so that you will probably miss about 30 seconds of the program itself. You will also experience 25- to 30-second lapses when, for dramatic effect, the program itself fades to black between scenes. Commercial eliminators range in price from $50 to as high as $350.

Cable TV converters. Although most VCRs are advertised as being capable of recording one channel while you are viewing another, problems exist if one of those channels is a numbered channel and the other is one of the lettered channels coming in on a cable system. The problem arises from the different types of signals being broadcast. Several of the newer TV models convert the lettered channels to UHF channels to facilitate remote-control operation. If this kind of conversion is not built into your set, it is possible to purchase a special converter for about $70. An alternative, as described in Chapter 4, is to obtain another converter box from the cable company and hook it up to your VCR. This will almost certainly involve an additional monthly rental charge. Still a third solution is a switching device which electronically switches the cable company's converter box from the VCR to the TV, or vice versa.

Switching devices. Most of the components discussed in this book—VCRs, video games, computers, cable TV, videodisc players—connect fairly easily to a standard TV set's antenna terminals. However, if more than two or three of these are hooked up at the same time, one can envision certain problems, both in esthetics and in logistics. Imagine, for example, trying to hold all of the component terminals in place while screwing down the antenna terminals.

A compact, easy-to-use tele-cine kit. AKAI AMERICA LTD.

There are now available several systems consisting of small, neat, out-of-the-way boxes. The box is hooked up to the antenna terminals and all of the other devices are then hooked up to the box. It then becomes a simple matter of turning the appropriate switch on and/or off. Such switching systems can also be used for switching the VCR from one TV set to another, switching the TV from one VCR to another, and a whole variety of combinations. The more complex and sophisticated switching devices are currently available for about $180; less expensive ones are available, but they are also less versatile.

Stabilizers. Motion pictures that are copied onto videotape cassettes for commercial sale or rental are encoded to avoid copying. With TV sets that have no "vertical hold" control (considered unnecessary because of automatic synchronization systems) this encoding can cause a rolling effect. Stabilizers, selling for $100 or less, are ostensibly designed to eliminate this problem. "But somehow," says the highly regarded video writer David Lachenbruch, "I suspect this isn't the principal use of these stabilizers—because they also make it possible to copy an encoded cassette onto another tape. This is known as piracy and is illegal." (*Panorama* Magazine, November 1980)

Audio improvers. Many TV sets and virtually all VCRs are made with a jack for plugging in earphones or other audio equipment. If your unit is so equipped, you can purchase a low-cost connector that plugs into the audio or earphone output jack of the TV or VCR and connects to your existing hi-fi system. A totally independent speaker/amplifier can also be connected in this way.

An interesting variation on this theme is TeleSound. This unit plugs into the VCR's audio jack. A single compact cabinet that fits easily on top of the VCR or a bookshelf contains a headphone jack, bass and treble controls, volume, and balance for simulated stereo. The simulation is accomplished by picking up the audio and playing it back through two speakers. The unit sells for about $130 and is available from TeleSound, Dept. VM-3, 88 Orchard Road CN-5219, Princeton, New Jersey 08540. Sylvania makes a monaural unit that operates on the same basic principles and lists for about $90.

Tele-cine (TC) adaptors. Once you own a VCR and a video camera, it is fairly easy, through the judicious employment of a TC adaptor, to convert home movies and slides to videocassettes for easier storage and display. These units are small, light, and simple to operate. The filmed material is projected in the usual way through a prism or a Fresnel lens onto a mirror, from which it is reflected into the video camera. The purpose of the prism or the Fresnel lens is to minimize the intensity of the light source. (Remember what happens to the vidicon tube in the camera if it is exposed to direct bright light.)

Quasar makes a TC adaptor that sells for about $130, and Akai recently announced a unit that sells for about $90. No doubt others will be appearing on the market very soon. In the meantime, if you prefer not to do this yourself, the Fotomat photofinishing establishments, as well as a number of video dealers, can provide the service for you.

Timing devices and techniques. Although all VCRs are equipped with digital counters, it is difficult to relate the number on the counter to specific recording or playing times. There is no uniformity among different brands of VCRs. Indeed, there is frequently no uniformity among various models of the same brand. There are several solutions to this problem. The least expensive, but also the most tedious, is to work out your own log. Set the counter at 0, begin playing the cassette, and then record the numbers on the counter at various time intervals: 15 minutes, 30 minutes, 60 minutes, or whatever segments you prefer.

Another method is to purchase charts that someone else has prepared. Several innovators have compiled the data that relate VCR digital counters to time periods. There is a separate chart for each VCR. Such charts and tables are available from, among others, Video Information Systems, Inc., 78 East 56th Street, New York, New York 10022, and Pacifica Labs, P.O. Box 813, Tarzana, California 91356.

The most sophisticated and expensive technique is an automatic timer that connects directly to the VCR and displays the length of time—in hours and minutes instead of the arbitrary numbers of the counter—that the tape has been played or recorded. These cost about $60.

Tripods and shoulder braces. The advantages and uses of a tripod have already been discussed in Chapter 8, as have the disadvantages of lightweight cameras. There is a wide variety of tripods and shoulder braces that can help to steady a camera. Prices vary, depending on the construction and sophistication of the unit. Tripods and shoulder braces should be purchased in person. It is the only way to test them for weight, comfort, and ease of operation.

Titling kits. Titles can be added to your videotapes in the same way they can be added to home movies. Strictly speaking, almost anything with a set of letters constitutes a titling kit. You may want to check the local camera store or video dealer for some fancy and sophisticated ones. Again, prices vary greatly. A basic kit can probably be purchased for $10 or $12.

Bulk erasers. These are devices that quickly and completely erase a videotape in a matter of seconds, eliminating the need to run the tape through a VCR. They are priced at about $50. Magnetic bulk erasers come in several types. Some require the insertion of the cassette into the unit and then a slow removal. Others consist of a cylinderlike device that is passed over the cassette. The chief advantage of the latter is that it can also be used for audio cassettes.

Splicing and cleaning kits. Several kits, in various price ranges, are available to facilitate the splicing of videotape. There are also kits, complete with swabs and cleaning fluids, for cleaning video heads. I maintain, however, that head cleaning, beyond the use of a head cleaning cassette, is best left to experts and technicians.

Caption converter. One of the most useful and important accessories ever invented is a special decoder that can be purchased for about $250 in Sears, Roebuck and Co., stores. NBC, ABC, PBS, and some cable and independent channels broadcast a special signal which, when picked up and transmitted through the decoder, provides captions on the screen for viewers with impaired hearing. Programs that are so captioned are labelled "CC" in the TV listings.

Cases. If you plan to do much travelling with your video equipment, you should give serious consideration to acquiring some proper cases. There are hundreds of cases available, ranging from cheap plastic shoulder bags (commonly known as gadget bags) on sale at photo-supply and video stores, to highly sophisticated, custom-made jobs. Virtually any piece of video equipment can be encased, including cameras, VCRs, and computers. Most case manufacturers stock units that are specifically designed for specific pieces of equipment from specific manufacturers. Some companies can custom design a case to suit your particular needs. All of these cases are designed for professional use and abuse; they are not, therefore, cheap. There are far too many types and sizes to give any meaningful range of prices. A careful examination of one company's catalogue, however, reveals that virtually no item sells for under $100. Extensive lines of cases are manufactured by the following companies: Anvil Cases, Inc., P.O. Box 888, Rosemead, California 91770; Thermodyne, Inc., 1260 Yukon Avenue, Hawthorne, California 90250; and Savoy Leather Manufacturing Corp., 1039 Chestnut Street, Newton Upper Falls, Massachusetts 02164. There are many other manufacturers and suppliers of cases. If you have come to know and trust your video dealer, perhaps it would be better to check with him first. He may very well have exactly what you are looking for in stock or can order it for you with considerably greater ease and convenience than you can yourself.

Various and sundry. If you visit a video dealer or an electronic-supply store, you will probably be lured by the so-called rack items. You will find all kinds of accessories on sale, including labels, boxes, cases, cleaners, plugs, wires, and so forth. These items all fall under the general category of "useful things" and should not be overlooked. If you have more that a passing interest in video, it seems reasonable to assume that you have a passing interest in gadgets in general. It is likely, therefore, that once you peruse a dealer's rack, you will discover several useful things you did not know you needed until you saw them. You may as well indulge yourself. These items tend

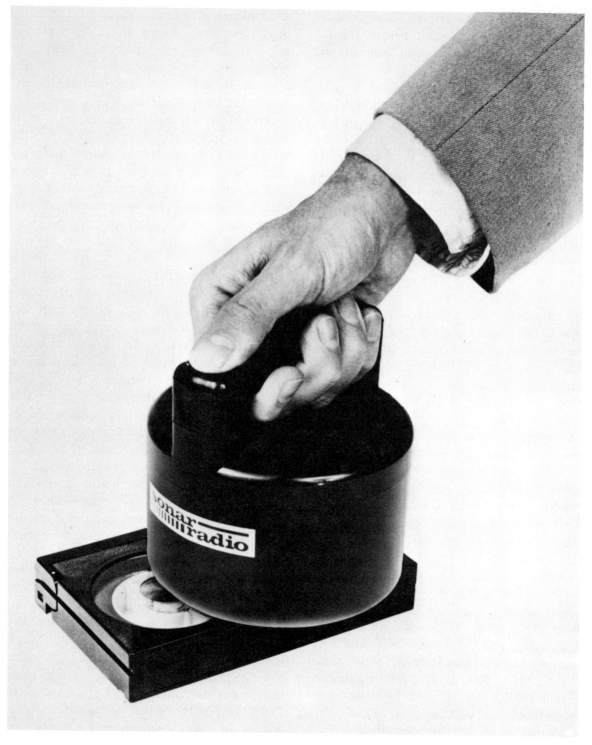

The Videoraser® will, according to the manu-facturer, completely erase videocassettes in seconds. SONAR RADIO CORP.

to be low in cost, fairly handy and convenient when you do use them, and they make your hobby a little more fun.

MICROPHONES

If you purchase a video camera, it is probably wise to get one that has a built-in microphone. There are several good reasons for doing so. First, you will have enough to do familiarizing yourself with the camera itself, without worrying about handling a separate piece of equipment like a microphone. Second, a built-in microphone means one less item that is likely to be left at home when you go shooting on location. And, third, there may be circumstances when a separate, external microphone is either unwieldy or inconvenient, or you may find it necessary and desirable to pick up the camera and shoot, with no time to plug in and manipulate a microphone.

The trouble with built-in microphones, however, is that they tend to be small and difficult to control. They are intended to serve as all-purpose audio pickups and offer little opportunity for selective sound recording.

After you have mastered the camera and want to become somewhat more selective in what you record, you may consider an external microphone. An excellent compromise between a built-in and an external mike is one that can be attached to the video camera so that it need not be held or manipulated separately but can be removed as circumstances dictate.

Once you own a microphone, it can be used for still another highly satisfying purpose. Virtually all VCRs have an input capability for dubbing sound onto the videotape. (*Dubbing* means adding sound some time after the picture has been recorded.) Decent microphones can be obtained for about $25 and up, so this is a relatively inexpensive way of vastly improving home videotapes of films, slide shows, and other personal presentations by writing a script and then dubbing in the narration. You can even add mood or background music and sound effects. (Some of these techniques are discussed in Chapter 10.)

The discussion of microphone types that follows involves the general construction of the elements that pick up the sound. Actual configurations of microphones—of almost any type—can differ considerably. There are, for example, lavalier mikes that are worn around a speaker's or singer's neck like a necklace. There are also tie-clip types which, as the name suggests, clip onto clothing. There are microphones that stand on tables, microphones that stand on poles, and microphones that are suspended from overhead booms. The type of configuration you want depends on the degree of sophistication you want to achieve and what circumstances and needs dictate. For the purpose of this book, we will assume that the interest is primarily in hand-held microphones that can be fitted to accessory stands or clipped onto cameras and are easy to operate.

The principle behind every microphone is the same. Sound waves enter the microphone and set up a series of vibrations. These vibrations are transformed into electrical impulses that are then transmitted to a recording medium. The electrical pulses are entered onto the recording medium in the form of magnetism and later, during playback, the process is reversed and sound emerges. Microphones contain a *diaphragm* which vibrates in reaction to the sound waves. They also contain a *transducer,* a unit that is sensitive to the vibration of the diaphragm and produces the electrical impulses. Generally, it is the transducer that differentiates one type of microphone from another.

Condenser microphone. A condenser microphone has an electrically charged conductor in the diaphragm. The vibration of the conductor produces variations in electrical voltage. According to some experts, condenser mikes are probably the best kind for

Unidirectional dynamic microphone. SHURE
BROTHERS, INC.

general video use, but they tend to be expensive and, because of their size, offer only limited portability.

Electret condenser. This is similar to the condenser type except that the charge in the conductor is a permanent one. These microphones generally offer a highly satisfactory recording range and are available at $50 to $100. Electret condenser mikes do require some care in extreme heat and high humidity.

Ceramic, crystal, piezoelectric. These contain ceramic or crystal elements that produce an electrical signal when the element is affected by the vibration of the diaphragm. These are usually the least expensive types available. The quality of their sound reproduction, however, is reflected in their price.

Dynamic. Dynamic microphones have a diaphragm attached to a coiled wire, known as a voice coil. This coil is placed in close proximity to a magnet. The vibration of the diaphragm causes the voice coil to move, and the combination of the coil and the magnet results in electrical output. At a price range of $50 to $100, dynamic microphones offer fairly good quality, a moderate price, and a reasonable amount of durability.

Microphone range. Most microphones are directional. A *unidirectional* mike picks up sound from whatever it is being pointed at. A *bidirectional* microphone picks up sounds from two different sources on either side of the microphone. *Omnidirectional* microphones pick up sounds in a circular manner, of which the microphone is the center. The radius of the circle depends on the sensitivity of the microphone. One type of omnidirectional microphone is the *cardioid,* so called because the outline of its pickup area is somewhat heart-shaped.

For most general uses, a good omnidirectional microphone will suffice. If spoken into at a fairly close range, the likelihood is that most of the background noises will be subdued. Even so, the sound quality is not quite as good as with a unidirectional microphone. On the other hand, if you want to record an

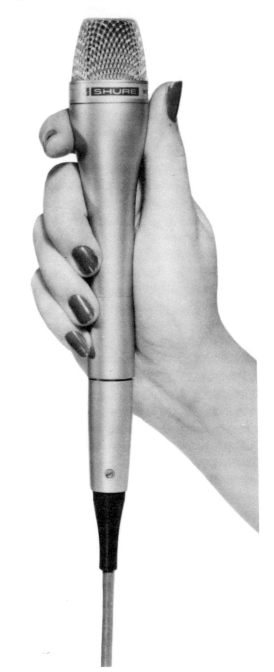

An omnidirectional dynamic microphone which, because of its light weight, is well suited for home video. SHURE BROTHERS, INC.

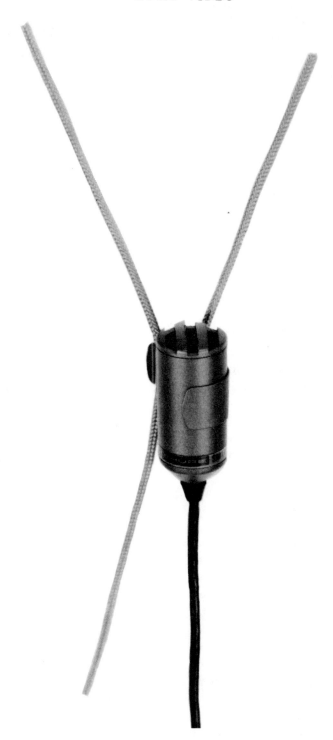

This dynamic omnidirectional microphone (actual size) is a lavalier type; it is worn around the speaker's or singer's neck. SHURE BRO-THERS, INC.

event with many people involved, an omnidirectional mike is ideal. There are situations where both would be useful. For example, you might want a unidirectional microphone to record a performer and an omnidirectional one to record audience reaction.

At that point, in addition to being a camera operator, you are becoming a sound mixer, regulating the input of the audio portion so that one element does not dominate the other. Good sound mixing requires good sound-mixing equipment, and if you are ready for that you are also ready for a book that is beyond this beginner's guide. (You will find several such books listed in the Bibliography beginning on page 153.)

Should you decide to use an accessory microphone outdoors, you should purchase a *windscreen*. Wind blowing across the surface of the microphone causes disturbing sounds that interfere with proper audio recording. A windscreen is a kind of sleeve or glove, usually made of a substance similar to foam rubber, that, as the name suggests, screens out the wind while permitting other sounds to come through.

BUY OR RENT?

Sometimes what is essential equipment for one person may only be an accessory for another. For example, you may decide that you really do not need to own a video camera since you plan to tape only very special, once-in-a-lifetime events, such as a wedding (although these days regarding a wedding as a once-in-a-lifetime event entails a certain degree of optimism), a special anniversary, or some other occasion that is not likely to be repeated soon. You might then decide that it would be nice to have the entire family, or a large group of friends, over to see the tape and that the best way to show it to them would be on a projection TV. It is worth keeping in mind that virtually any piece of equipment that can be bought can also be rented. There are many rental outlets that can

supply equipment. You can probably find them by leafing through the Yellow Pages. In a pinch, contact companies that rent audiovisual equipment. They can either supply the video equipment you need or they can tell you who does. Similarly, many video retailers either have rental facilities or can refer you to some.

You can also take advantage of a fairly new business that is cropping up all over the country. Many commercial photographers now offer videotaping services as an alternative to film. They have the equipment, the skill, and the experience to provide a videocassette that can be played on your own VCR. There are even some entrepreneurs who specialize in videotaping. Their services are not cheap, but it makes sense to make use of them if you plan to actively participate in the event. It also makes sense to rent a piece of equipment that you are likely to need only once or twice a year at most. (Incidentally, it should be mentioned in passing that ordinary TV sets can be rented for various periods of time, for guest rooms, sick rooms, and so forth.)

ELECTRONICS FURNITURE

It is difficult to pinpoint the exact moment in history when ordinary cabinets and bookcases made the transition to electronics furniture. It probably occurred about the time hi-fi audio equipment became a craze. It became fashionable among hi-fi buffs to accumulate their own systems, with a turntable from one manufacturer, amplifiers and speakers from another, tuners from yet another, and so on. Soon a person whose audio equipment could simulate the sound of a freight train passing through the living room was confronted with a collection of boxes strung together by an assortment of wires closely resembling several pounds of week-old spaghetti. It did not take long for enterprising business people to design cabinets to house all of this stuff, and the electronics furniture industry was in full swing.

Clearly, a parallel situation is developing

An example of electronics furniture, this unit holds an assortment of video and audio equip- *ment in an attractive and readily accessible cabinet.* GUSDORF CORP.

This convenient cabinet houses a TV, a video-cassette recorder, and even provides storage space for the most actively used video cassettes. GUSDORF CORP.

with respect to home video. A collection comprising anything that could be called a home video system would include a TV set with remote control and a VCR. Possibly a videodisc player could be added. In addition, most homes that are so equipped are also likely to have an audio system, with its speakers, tuners, and all the rest. It is easy to visualize a hodgepodge of metal and plastic boxes strung out around a living room—unless, of course, you have electronics furniture.

Michael Wirtman, vice president of the Gusdorf Corporation, claims that "electronics furniture is sized to conform to the dimensions of the equipment. In fact, we're privy to the latest introductions in audio and video equipment, so that we can engineer the furniture to match their specifications." His company—as well as several others—offers tables, stands, and cabinets that are designed to house various electronic components in compact, attractive settings. So prolific is the home-entertainment industry that Wirtman predicts that in the near future homes will have a "media" room that "needs to be as well furnished as it is equipped with electronic paraphernalia."

For those who want total video but are unwilling to invest the time in putting everything together, this Magnavox "Performing Arts Center" may be the answer. It includes a 3-tube 50-inch projection TV, the Magnavision video- *disc player, a 19-inch portable TV, a 6-hour VHS VCR, a color video camera, an electronic game system, and a complete audio system.* MAGNAVOX CONSUMER ELECTRONICS CO.

If you are handy, you can, of course, build your own furniture to house your electronic paraphernalia. Mr. Wirtman points out, however, that the furniture should have such safety features as removable panels that allow the equipment to breathe, carriers at the rear to prevent wires from tangling, and should be of sufficient sturdiness to handle the weight of the equipment. Acoustical considerations also enter into the construction. (Gusdorf, incidentally, takes credit for originating the term electronics furniture.)

Of course, any good furniture dealer can supply many types of cabinets, stands, and tables. If styling and design are more important than maximum efficiency of equipment operation, then you should buy whatever furniture best suits your tastes. There are those, however, who hold, with some justification, to the premise that expensive and efficient equipment should be housed in a manner that best supports, protects, displays, and takes advantage of that equipment, and electronics furniture does seem to answer these demands best. There is so much variety in styling, size, and configuration, including a number of modular systems, that it should be possible to find a satisfying compromise between design and function among the several lines of electronics furniture now available.

THE ULTIMATE ACCESSORY

Of all the complex and intricate devices designed to enhance the enjoyment of a home video system, my personal favorite is one that perhaps represents the ultimate in simplicity, utility, and durability at a price that is irresistible.

A compassionate and imaginative entrepreneur is offering for sale the "TV Brick." It is made of light, soft foam rubber, but it closely resembles a real brick. This item can rest on a table or the arm of a chair, in close proximity to the viewer, who, upon feeling an uncontrollable urge to react to something on the screen, lifts the object and heaves it mightily in the direction of the offense. It gives instant relief. It can be purchased for $5 each or $8 for two, plus $1 for shipping, from Universal Enterprises, Merritt Island, Florida. No home should be without one.

10

Producing Your Own TV Program

You bid me make it orderly and well,
According to the fashion and the time.

—The Taming of the Shrew, IV, iii

Don't get excited.

The title of this chapter is not intended to suggest that you undertake the supervision of some new and inane situation comedy that will be broadcast over the length and breadth of the Republic under the sponsorship of a manufacturer of detergents or tampons. As you may recall from the first few pages of this book, "program" refers to anything you look at on a TV screen.

"Producing" means putting together something that no one has ever seen before. For the most part, these are likely to be events and situations of a personal nature: weddings, bar mitzvahs, school plays, amateur sporting events, vacations, parties, and various other activities in your life, both public and private. The productions we are talking about are meant entirely for the pleasure, delectation, or improvement of yourself, your friends, and your relatives. They are therefore limited only by your way of life and your discretion.

That does not mean that you could not or should not be creative. If you have the inclination and the time, there is no reason why you cannot produce what amounts to an original TV play or a video documentary. It will stretch a home video system to its very limits to produce such a program at a level of quality that would be worthy of public broadcasting, but that should not discourage you. After all, few amateur theatrical groups are ready for Broadway, but that does not prevent them from having a very good time while putting on plays.

The fact that your production is an amateur one is never an excuse for a program that is boring, difficult to watch because it was badly photographed, and incomprehensible or unintelligible because it is poorly organized. You have sat through enough of other people's movies and slide shows to know that sloppy or thoughtless photography, coupled with indiscriminate displays of the entire output, foisted on an unsuspecting captive audience is enough to destroy once-beautiful friendships. The primary purpose of this chapter is to help you avoid going forth and doing likewise.

It is axiomatic that we learn in two ways: by being taught and by doing. When it comes to being taught, I am again compelled to recommend a working familiarity with one of the video magazines described in the Bibliography. In addition to up-to-date information on equipment and accessories, these publications invariably include at least one article on technique. Similarly, photography magazines can offer a good deal of useful information because many of the techniques and methods used for effective photography work equally well in videotaping. As a matter of fact, a few hours spent with a good photography text that deals at length with composition will yield many rewarding video images for you.

Have no qualms about adopting or adapting a technique that someone else uses successfully. Try to develop a critical and observant eye when watching TV shows. You will soon discover that there are a number of little tricks and techniques (some of which we'll be discussing shortly) that professionals employ for smooth transitions, dramatic effects, and variety. You may even want to take notes during a program to record those effects you particularly like and would like to try. Here, by the way, is an especially creative use for a VCR: If you are aware that some particular series consistently uses photographic techniques that you want to emulate, you could

Camera angle changes the overall picture significantly. By choosing a low angle, the camera operator eliminates unwanted background, gives added height to the subject and the action, and emphasizes the subject's attributes. AKAI AMERICA, LTD.

record one or two programs and then review them using the "pause" and "freeze-frame" capabilities of the VCR to study composition, lighting techniques, and camera handling.

THINGS TO DO IN ADVANCE

Before you actually begin taping what you hope will be an interesting and diverting program, there are some things that should be done in advance.

Know your equipment. If you are planning to tape a once-in-a-lifetime event, the event itself is the wrong time to discover that you are not sure where certain controls are or what they do. The ideal to strive for is the ability to operate your equipment—especially your video camera and portable VCR—in the dark. (Of course, it will do you no good to actually operate them in the dark; we are talking about a principle and not actual practice.) Practically speaking, you will be greatly hampered if you must remove your eye from the viewfinder in order to adjust some control on the camera or the VCR. It is essential, therefore, that you know at least the basic controls, where they are, what they do, and when to use them.

Similarly, you should learn the capabilities and limitations of your equipment. If you are filming a wedding scene, you should know that you cannot expect to pick up the words of the minister with a built-in microphone if you are taking a long shot down the aisle. A quick look at the ambient lighting will let you know, well in advance, which scenes you are likely to photograph correctly and which ones are likely to be under-exposed. You should know how close you can move in with the lens you are using before the picture becomes blurred and distorted beyond recognition.

Once you are familiar with these limitations, they can themselves become creative tools. Distortion, lack of critical focus, very low lighting, the absence or presence of sound —all can be used for special, often dramatic, effects. Remember that the one main advantage that videotape has over film is its reusability. Designate one or two cassettes as those that you will wear out through constant experimentation and testing. What can you lose by photographing your black-and-white Dalmatian with a green filter over the lens other than, perhaps, a little loyalty on the dog's part?

Once you have become thoroughly familiar with your equipment, you can consider making an actual production. There are some preparations that should be made ahead of time.

A shooting script. With rare exception, to achieve a smooth, interesting, and enjoyable finished production at least some editing will probably be required. There are some people who enjoy editing. I have always found it to be something of a nuisance; it is akin to proofreading a printed page. As you will see when we discuss editing at length later in this chapter, it is not easy to edit a videocassette and there is always the danger of the final production looking choppy and pieced together.

The most effective way to minimize editing is to begin with a shooting script. Most people tend to think of a script as the meticulously written out document in which every line of dialogue and every picture is carefully delineated. For our purposes, however, we may think of the script as a basic shooting program. It simply means that by planning the shots and the probable sequence in which they will be made, the entire procedure will be easier, faster, more efficient, and better organized.

With the possible exception of vacations in places where you have never been before, you are likely to have a fairly good idea of what to expect in advance of any shooting situation.

One of the greatest inventions ever devised for use by creative people is the simple and ubiquitous index card. Write down on a separate card each sequence or portion of an event that you want to record. If your child is going to appear in a school play, for example, you might want a set of cards that reads:

CHILD PUTTING ON COSTUME
EXTERIOR SHOT OF SCHOOL BUILDING
LONG SHOT OF STAGE
MEDIUM SHOT OF STAGE SHOWING CHILD
   IN GROUP
CLOSE-UP OF CHILD PERFORMING SOLO
OVERALL VIEW OF AUDIENCE REACTIONS
CLOSEUP SHOT OF MOTHER WITH TEAR
   IN EYE

Once you have all of the likeliest scenes written down, you can then arrange the cards in the sequence in which those scenes are likely to occur or likely to be shot. For example, it will probably be easier to shoot several of the stage scenes at one time and several of the audience reactions at one time, even though those scenes are likely to be interspersed throughout the finished production. If you are not sure of the sequence of occurrences, you can almost always check in advance with someone who is likely to know, like a faculty advisor at a school or a sexton at a church wedding. Note, however, that "in advance" does not mean five minutes before curtain time. Most people involved with events will willingly cooperate with you a day or two before the event is scheduled to take place.

After you have the cards arranged in the desired sequence, transfer the information to a somewhat more portable and convenient medium, such as a small notebook or even a single sheet of paper that you can carry in your pocket. Take it along with you and use it as a checklist.

Of course, your script can be as detailed and complicated as you wish, especially if it is totally within your control. The more detailed the script, the more likely that the finished production will resemble what you had in mind at the start. You may even want to consider using a *TV storyboard*. This is a sheet on which is printed a number of frames resembling blank TV screens. In each of the frames you can sketch an approximation of the picture you want to capture. There is space beneath each frame for captions and notes. You can make your own storyboard or you can buy blanks for a pittance in almost any art-supply store.

In any case, don't be too rigidly controlled by the script. Unless you are shooting a carefully planned and rehearsed event, you should be prepared for surprises, unusual occurrences, and interesting but unplanned scenes. It is often difficult to anticipate with precision what animals and/or children are likely to do at any given time. The same is true for adults with a propensity for behaving like animals or children. Be prepared for anything.

Preparation. Check out everything before the time to shoot arrives. Make sure, for example, that all connectors and equipment are functioning properly, that batteries are either fresh or fully charged, and that your cassettes are in working order. If you plan to do your shooting at some location away from home, prepare a checklist well in advance of everything you will need or want. In fact, such a checklist could be a permanent reference tool for use on location shootings. Check each item as you pack it and then go over the list again to make sure you have everything.

Estimate the amount of tape you think you will need and take along at least double the quantity. This will provide you with an ample supply in case a cassette jams or circumstances tempt you to shoot more than you originally intended. This will also prevent you from experiencing the constraints of tape conservation brought on by the fear of running out of tape before you run out of event. Remember that you cannot shoot too much tape because you can always erase and reuse what you later decide you do not want.

Lighting. If at all possible, check out the lighting prior to the event, especially if you expect to be shooting indoors. The prevailing light level may simply be too low for decent videotaping. If so, determine whether supplementary lighting can be used. For about $50 or $60 you can rent portable lights that may be attached to the camera. Many religious institutions, however, do not permit the use of such lights during actual ceremonies. Indeed, several do not even permit filming or taping in sanctuaries or of religious ceremonies. It is easy to check in advance and doing so can save you considerable embarrassment.

If you decide to use portable lighting, remember that the average battery power pack lasts only about half an hour. Either come supplied with additional power packs or use an AC adaptor. Should you decide on the latter, you will have to make sure that you have enough extension cords to give you the necessary mobility. You will also have to make sure that you do not become a hazard with your extension cords. Consider engaging the services of an assistant whose responsibilities are to see that none of the guests or participants is electrocuted or tripped up by your extension cords. Such services are often obtainable from a family member through various techniques, including cajolery, guilt, and bribery.

In general, try to keep the lighting as natural to the situation and as pleasing to the viewer as possible. In an outdoor location, the dappled effect achieved by the sun filtering through leaves may look romantic to you, but it is often disturbing and uncomfortable when viewed as a picture. Strong sunlight may show up colors and outlines clearly, but it may also cause subjects to squint. (Professional photographers discovered long ago that for outdoor pictures of people open shade is probably the best all-around lighting.)

When shooting indoors, use existing light whenever possible. If supplementary lighting is needed for ordinary home scenes (as opposed to staged dramatic scenes), inexpensive photoflood lamps, available at most photo shops, should do the trick. There are several methods for using photofloods. One of the simplest is to remove the lightbulbs in the lamps and fixtures already in the room and replace them with photoflood bulbs. Within a very short time everyone in the room will become thoroughly accustomed to the new and increased lighting. (In fact, people often comment on how dark the room looks when normal lighting is restored.)

Photofloods can also be used in simple fixtures that are affixed to clamps. These clamps can then be attached to the backs of chairs, on doors, coatracks, and so forth. Also available at very low cost are metal reflectors which fit easily onto the clamp-on fixtures, making it possible to direct and control the light.

There are a couple of precautions to be observed when using photofloods. For one thing, these bulbs become extremely hot. Avoid touching them when they are on and allow them to cool for a few minutes after they have been turned off. If a hot photoflood lamp is touched by metal, such as a ring, it is likely to shatter.

If you decide to bathe the entire room in photoflood light by pointing the reflectors at the ceiling, be careful to note the color of the ceiling. If it is white, off-white, or light gray, there should be no problem. But if the ceiling is painted some other color—yellow, blue, green, or a shade of red—the reflected light will be dominated by that color. You may be able to compensate for it by means of the color controls on your camera or with a corrective filter.

SOME BASIC TAPING TECHNIQUES

The two most common causes of poor pictures are *movement* and *selective focusing*.

Movement. The slightest movement of the camera is greatly exaggerated when seen on a screen. If you place a camera on a car door to capture the landscape as you drive by, you will wind up with a shaking, jiggling picture that is likely to make your audience seasick. A number of factors, including peripheral vision, help the human brain adjust to such conditions when actually on the scene, but the camera can make no such adjustment and the result can often be disastrous.

Even slight hand tremors or the general unsteadiness of the camera operator can cause annoying distractions on the screen. These movements become far worse as the camera moves in closer to the subject, either physically or with a zoom or telephoto lens. The only antidote for an unsteady hand is a tripod or shoulder brace.

Selective focusing. Selective focusing is a quality that every functioning human brain has and that no camera comes equipped with. It is the ability to focus—really, to concentrate—on what you want to see to the practical, if not actual, exclusion of everything else.

Imagine that you are planning to shoot a subject who is looking contemplative and beatific in the midst of an exquisitely beautiful sylvan setting, surrounded, perhaps, by apple blossoms. Your subject's expression is perfect, the color is perfect, and the overall setting is simply gorgeous. You carefully and lovingly make your shot and, when you see it later on the screen, you discover that the subject appears to have a branch, laden with apple blossoms, passing directly through the ears.

Selective focusing is the culprit. The eye saw the branch of the tree, but the brain did not register it because it was concentrating on the subject. The camera, however, has no brains and it therefore records everything with equal objectivity.

The only way to cure selective focusing is through practice. After a while you will be able to look at everything that appears in the viewfinder to see whether unwanted branches, light poles, lamps, your own shadow, or busy and distracting backgrounds are interfering with the ideal and idyllic composition you want to achieve.

Another danger caused by selective focusing is unintentional amputation. Try to avoid cutting off various ends of people unless you are doing so specifically for dramatic effect. Missing tops of heads, feet that have been amputated at the ankles, and hands that have been cut off at the wrists make for disturbing compositions.

Of course, you cannot always show the entire body, nor should you want to. The trick is to avoid performing photographic surgery in those places where actual amputation might be likely to occur. In general, avoid ending your picture at the joints. If, for example, you cannot include the entire arm, cut it off somewhere between the shoulder and the elbow, or between the elbow and the wrist, rather than *at* the shoulder, elbow, or wrist. The same applies to the ankle, knee, and crotch. If you want a medium-range or closeup shot of someone, do your amputation at the bust line or just above or below it rather than at the waist. Again, with a little practice you will soon become adept at pleasing photographic dismemberment.

Positioning. After movement and selective focusing, the most common photographic failing among amateurs is distance. Look through some of your old family snapshots. You will very likely find that many of them consist of tiny figures in the center of a print or slide, surrounded by dull or irrelevant landscape.

Don't be afraid to move in close, either physically or with a zoom lens. With most lenses you can probably get as close as five or six feet. (With many lenses, however, this can cause a marked distortion in facial features. This problem does not exist with zoom lenses.)

If you are photographing two or more people, get them close together. This may appear a little strange and even awkward, but it will show up well on television. The distances that people normally keep during such activity as conversation tend to make them appear to be too far apart on a TV screen.

Much can be accomplished by a simple shift of the camera angle. A low angle, for example, can make someone seem exceptionally tall; conversely, a high angle can diminish, both physically and psychologically, the appearance of the subject. You can even tilt the camera a little for special dramatic effects.

In general, the best camera position is one that is at the same approximate eye level as the subject. This gives the audience a natural and comfortable point of view. Unless you are trying for some special dramatic impact, it is virtually mandatory that when photographing children you get down to their level. You may have to kneel, sit, or even lie down flat. Do it. The results will be worth it.

Space. I know it is difficult to think of such things when you are actually making pictures, but try to conceive of the composition of a picture in terms of taking a number of elements and placing them in some kind of arrangement within an empty space in such a way as to convey some kind of message to someone looking at the final result. By "message" I mean whatever notion or idea you want to project, even a pretty landscape or an interesting face. Imagine that there are cross hairs drawn horizontally and vertically through your viewfinder. This separates the

An interesting face deserves an extreme close-up (ECU). Don't be afraid to move in, especi- *ally if you have a zoom lens.* GENEREAL ELEC-TRIC.

viewfinder into four exactly equal rectangles. Where the imaginary cross hairs meet is the precise center of your picture. When you know where that precise center is, avoid placing the main object of your picture at the center. More pleasing compositions usually result when the main object is placed above or below and to the right or the left of dead center. That doesn't mean your subject should be tucked away in a corner somewhere. Nor does it mean that there are never occasions when this rule cannot, or should not, be broken. But with the cross hair concept in mind you may find it a little easier to "construct" your picture and avoid static, clunky-looking images. It will not be necessary to keep this principle

in mind all the time. With a little practice it will become second nature.

It is important to leave room for the people in your picture to perform their actions. If you are shooting a baseball player at bat, leave room in front of him to swing. If, by some stroke of luck, he should actually hit the ball, there must be room for that ball to move into. Even if you are taking a close-up of someone who is not facing the camera directly, leave some room for that person to look into. Many film makers refer to this as nose room.

Nose room not only allows for better composition; it has a practical use, too. If it becomes necessary to keep a subject in the viewfinder as he or she moves, and if that

By moving in close to an object in a subject's hands and then panning slowly along the arms to the face, a dramatic, story-telling sequence results. SONY CORP. OF AMERICA.

For the most pleasing results, photograph peo- ple at eye level. If necessary, get down on the ground to photograph children and/or animals. GENERAL ELECTRIC.

movement is rapid—as might be the case at a sporting event—by providing adequate nose room you are less likely to have the subject move out of the viewfinder. Remember that your object is to have the camera follow your subject, not chase him.

As long as we are on the subject of movement, this seems a good place to talk about panning. If you stand in one place and follow a subject by moving the camera, you are panning. Panning is also used to depict a broad, sweeping scene. The camera starts at one end and pans across the city skyline, the mountain

range, the entire wedding party, or the beautiful furnishings inside a room. The only thing worse than looking at a motion picture that has been made from a moving car is looking at one in which the camera operator has panned too quickly. It causes blurred vision, headaches, and extreme irritation. It is also a complete waste of film or tape, because the viewer has no idea what you are trying to show.

To be effective, panning must be done *very, very* slowly. If you want to be on the safe side, have someone time you while you do a dry run of the pan. Then, when you are ready to actually record the scene, at least double the amount of time you thought was enough to get it all in.

There is, however, one justification for fast panning. Called swish panning, it is an effective method of making a transition from one scene to another. In swish panning you focus on one subject until the desired action has been recorded and then rapidly pan across to the second subject. The material that is recorded during the panning will appear as nothing more than a blur. It is a very effective method for suggesting speed and fast action. It should be used judiciously, however, especially since there are a number of other effective transition methods.

Transition. A transition is a means of getting from one scene to the next.

Jump cut. This is the simplest technique. When you are finished recording the desired action, you simply stop the camera and then begin taping the next action. It is a method that is both useful and simple, but excessive use gives the finished product a somewhat shoddy and definitely amateurish appearance. It can also be confusing, because it is best to give your audience a few seconds to adjust to the idea that one scene has ended and another scene is about to begin.

Walk-through. This gives the appearance of the camera passing through some solid object or of a person walking "through" the camera. Here is how it works: Suppose you are taping a sequence of a child getting into a costume for a play. At the end of the sequence the child walks directly toward the camera until his or her body completely blocks the lens. The next sequence *opens* with the *back* of the child's body blocking the lens. The child is then seen walking away from the camera, perhaps to the car or onto the stage.

The reverse of the walk-through involves the movement of the camera rather than the subject. In the same production, for example, the camera moves slowly down the aisle of the auditorium, closer and closer to the curtain, until the curtain completely blocks the lens. The next sequence opens with the inside of the curtain completely blocking the lens and the camera backs away to reveal the activity on the stage before the curtain rises.

Fade. If your video camera has a fade control, it is easy to end the scene by fading to black and beginning the next scene by starting with black and then fading into the action. If there is no such control on the camera, a similar effect can be achieved by operating the camera's iris or diaphragm. This is a little tricky and requires a small amount of practice and some degree of manual dexterity. At the end of the scene the iris is closed down to its smallest opening so that the scene darkens considerably. As the next scene begins, the iris is gradually opened to create the fade-in effect. Care must be taken, however, not to open the iris too far, or the subsequent scene will be over-exposed.

Focus. A scene can be ended by deliberately throwing the lens out of focus so that the image becomes completely blurred. As the next scene begins, it opens with an unfocused view and the lens is gradually refocused for a sharp image. The same practice and manual dexterity required for iris manipulation in fades is required here.

EDITING

There are three good reasons for editing. First, editing provides for a smooth, near-professional production by eliminating badly exposed or photographed sequences, boring redundancies, and confusing irrelevancies. Second, it permits the arrangement of sequences in such a way as to achieve a dramatic or logical result. And, third, it is the only sensible way to assemble related material for easier viewing. For example, the only way to demonstrate how or whether someone's golf game has improved is to accumulate scenes from various cassettes over a period of time and place those scenes in a chronological sequence on a single cassette. (Here is a rather nice

An example of nose room. There is sufficient room in front of the horse's nose for the animal to complete the jump without seeming to leap out of the picture. GENERAL ELECTRIC.

touch you may want to try: On each of your child's birthdays take fifteen or twenty seconds of tape showing a close-up of the child's face. Then, after a few years, transfer all of the takes to a single cassette in chronological order. You will then have a tape that shows, in a dramatic, pleasing, and even amusing way, the growth and development of your child.)

Before launching into a detailed discussion of editing, I should point out that a number of different kinds of assemblages, known as editing decks, are available. These are costly, complicated, and usually designed for reel-to-reel tape rather than for cassettes. Once again, if you plan to produce programs of professional quality, you may want to consider the acquisition of an editing deck. We will continue to confine our discussion here to editing with a home video system.

Editing videotape requires considerable patience and dedication. It also requires two

A variation of nose room: When following action, leave room in front of the subject. This skier has plenty of room to move into. Also, *it is easier to keep the subject in the viewfinder when taping.* GENERAL ELECTRIC.

VCRs. Many people who have reached the stage where they want to edit their productions probably already have two VCRs—the deck or console type which remains, more or less permanently, in one place, and a portable unit that is used in conjunction with a video camera. If you have never done editing before and do not own a second VCR, please do not rush out to buy one. Borrow or rent the second unit and avoid making any purchases until you are certain that you want to be a videotape editor.

The principal difference between tape editing and film editing is fairly obvious. With film you can see what you are doing simply by examining the frames, either through a film editor or by holding the film up to the light. You can then make such cuts and splices as are necessary and where they are appropriate. A clean splice on film, when done with skill, care, and practice, can be invisible in the final production. With tape it is an entirely different matter.

No matter how careful you are, you cannot really be sure that you are cutting the tape in precisely the right place. Furthermore, it is almost impossible to splice the tape so carefully that the break is not evident, at least a little.

There is really only one way to edit videotape: Start with a clean, unrecorded tape or one which has material on it that you no longer want to keep. Then record the scenes on that tape in the sequence in which you want them to appear. Here is a relatively simple, if slightly tedious, step-by-step method for editing videotape cassettes.

1. Set the digital counter on your VCR at 0 and insert the cassette containing the scene or scenes you want to edit. Start running the VCR.

2. When you come to the scene you want to include, note the numbers on the digital counter and write them down on an index card, along with whatever designation you have given the cassette itself. Add a brief description to identify the scene. Make a separate card for each scene you want to include.

If these scenes exist in more than one cassette, then follow this procedure for each cassette, always remembering to set the digital counter at 0 before you begin playing the cassette.

3. Arrange the file cards in the sequence in which you want the scenes to appear in the final tape.

4. Connect the two VCRs. For the purposes of this discussion we will call the playback unit VCR A and the recording unit VCR B.

5. Insert the new cassette in VCR B and rewind it to "start."

6. In VCR A insert the cassette that is indicated on your first index card. Rewind or fast-forward this cassette to the proper position, as indicated by the digital counter.

7. Play back a portion of the sequence to be sure it is the one you want and then rewind it to the beginning of the sequence.

8. Set VCR A in the "playback" mode and VCR B in the "record" mode and record the scene you want. When the scene ends, activate the "stop" control on VCR B. Here is where your creativity comes in. Now is your chance to start or end the sequence somewhere other than where it originally starts or ends. Now is the time to shorten it and excise unnecessary and extraneous material.

9. Refer to the second index card. If that scene is on the cassette that is still in VCR A, locate it by using the method already described and record the second scene on VCR B. Otherwise remove the cassette in the first VCR and replace it with the one that contains the second scene.

10. Continue repeating the above procedure until you have a complete, edited production.

Usually a VCR requires a fraction of a second to operate at full speed. Because of this, you may find a slight picture distortion at the beginning and the end of each scene. These are called glitches. Glitches can sometimes be avoided by overlapping. If you use the "freeze-frame" feature on a VCR, you can "backspace" a frame or two and overlap the first frame or two of the next scene with the previous one. This tends to minimize the glitch. Even better, if possible use a portable VCR for the recording unit. These are less likely to produce glitches. However, even if you cannot eliminate glitches, they are a very small price to pay if the alternative is watching what seems to be interminably long, unedited videotapes which, at best, tend to lull viewers into a kind of stupor.

DUBBING

Unless, for some reason, it complicates matters, it is probably advisable to record the ambient sound at the same time that you are recording pictures. To be sure, you will probably wind up with sounds that you neither want nor need, but it is very easy to erase the unwanted audio portion of a video program. It is extremely difficult, however, to obtain a sound recording of something you have already missed.

The easiest and most effective way to get rid of *unwanted* sound is to record *wanted* sound over it. The process of adding sound to a video production after the pictures have been made is called *dubbing*. Mercifully, there is no need to go through anything like the process just described for editing. Once you have a completely edited cassette, you can simply add the sound to it by plugging a microphone into your VCR.

You can be as creative and interesting with sound as you can with pictures. One of the simplest and most effective techniques is a straight narration or, as it is known in the trade, a voice-over. Like the pictorial images, the narration should be smooth and natural. It should also be rehearsed. Run the cassette through your VCR and make notes as you watch the scenes. (Alternately, you could use the index cards that you used for the editing process.) Once you have a general idea of what you want to say about each of the

scenes, *write out* a script. Don't get fancy. Use language that you are familiar with and that your audience will understand. Rehearse the narration several times before you actually tape it. Then start recording. If you make a mistake, simply start over again,

When you write the narration, have a little respect for your audience's intelligence. There is almost never any need to explain or describe the obvious (a lesson most sports announcers have yet to learn). While it may be true that a picture is worth ten thousand words, it does not necessarily follow that ten thousand words are worth a picture. Let the pictures speak for themselves as much as possible. A line like, "As you can see, the mother of the elf has been moved to tears," is an affront both to your photography and the viewers' perceptions.

You may even want to add a little background music to your production. If you want *only* music, place your favorite record or audio cassette on your hi-fi system, plug in the audio system to your VCR, and, after determining—perhaps through a little trial and error—that you have the proper volume level, let the machines take over. If you want narration *and* music, have the audio system play the tape or record "behind" you as you speak. Here, too, you will have to play around a little to make sure that the music is loud enough to be heard but not so loud that it interferes with the voice.

Chances are that your VCR comes equipped with both a microphone jack and an "audio dub" facility. Refer to the instruction manual to determine the proper procedure for using these features. For example, if you decide to record music directly from your stereo system into the VCR, you may require special cables. If your instruction manual is not clear on this point, check with your video dealer or the local electronics-supply store.

While we have tended, in this book, to shy away from devices, techniques, and facilities best left to professionals, sound is one area in which you may want to emulate the experts.

Several companies offer, at varying cost, background music and sound effects. One such firm offers a catalogue totalling 152 pages that lists music covering such categories as action/agitated movements, comedy and cartoons, a veritable United Nations of ethnic music, marches, religious music, space music, wedding music, and so forth. These firms also offer sound effects that include cocktail parties, all sorts of clocks, cannon and other weaponry, horses, vehicles, machines, and so forth. Among the companies offering such delightful smorgasbords are Thomas J. Valentino, Inc., 151 West 46th Street, New York, New York 10036, and D. E. Wolfe Music Library, Inc., 25 West 45th Street, New York, New York 10036. There are many other firms —at least one or two are probably close to where you live—that provide similar services. These musical and sound effects are generally designed for industrial, professional, or commercial use and are therefore not cheap. They will, however, give you the music and sound you want and need as long as you are willing to pay the price.

HOME MOVIES AND SLIDES

The production techniques discussed in this chapter can all be applied to transferring slides and movie film to videotape. Obviously the editing should be done with the film before the transfer. With movie film a fairly simple combination editor/splicer unit can be purchased or rented. With slides it is simply a matter of arranging the slides in the desired sequence.

The actual transfer involves setting up the movie or slide projector, the screen, and then, using a video camera, making a tape of what is projected on the screen. This seemingly simple procedure, however, presents several problems. For one thing, a movie projector does not operate at a speed that is synchronized to the VCR, so some shaking or jumping may result.

Another problem may be caused by the failure to perfectly align the video camera with the projection screen, resulting in distortion. This difficulty is best eliminated by using rear-screen projection so that the camera and the projector can be perfectly aligned. It is important to be very careful that the projector is turned off before the screen is put into place or removed, because the bright light from the projector can damage or even destroy the camera's vidicon tube.

In the long run it is probably more economical and efficient—especially in terms of time —to use one of the tele-cine units described in the previous chapter. Once the movie or slides have been transferred to videotape, sound can be added in the manner previously described.

DUPLICATES

After the editing and dubbing are completed, the finished cassette should be clearly labelled with the title, subject, date, and any other identifying information, plus the words MASTER CASSETTE clearly and boldly marked. That master cassette should become your original and ought to be treated accordingly. The cassettes from which the scenes were lifted are known as the first generation. The edited master cassette is known as the second generation. Any copies made from the master cassette would constitute the third generation. Any copies made from that would represent the fourth generation, and so on. It is important to remember that with each generation there is a slight loss in both video and audio quality. It is therefore best to make copies only from the master. Also, as each showing tends to cause some slight deterioration of the tape, as long as you have two VCRs available, make your own third generation copy from your master to be used for frequent showings. You can save the master for making additional copies when your own third generation copy shows signs of wear.

OTHER PRODUCTIONS

Insurance. When you acquire your video system, one of your first productions should be a videotape recording of your home and everything in it.

Insurance tapes should be made on an average of once a year to show new acquisitions and any changes in the condition of your possessions. Check with your insurance broker. Your insurance company may have special pointers on making an insurance tape. Some firms even have pamphlets on how to do it. First record the exterior of your home and then the inside. Cover every room and everything of value in the room. Open and photograph drawers where jewelry and valuables are kept. Separate small objects so that they are clearly discernible. As you tape, have someone point out distinguishing features of objects such as nicks and scratches. Large objects should be taken from various angles; don't forget to move in close to show serial numbers and brand names.

It is a good idea to begin the tape with something that shows the date, like a copy of a newspaper. If possible, borrow or rent a video camera so that you can include your own video equipment on the tape.

Don't worry about a fancy production; just make sure that everything is included. With insurance tapes it is better to have too much than not enough.

It is important to bear in mind that a photographic or video record is not proof of ownership, so any sales slips or other documentation that you would normally retain for such proof should not be discarded. These documents and the tape should be stored someplace away from the home, ideally in a safe-deposit box.

Training. One of the most effective ways for people to improve their technique in some field of endeavor is to see themselves in action. I have seen this work for actors, musicians, public speakers, and athletes. The first attempts at taping someone in action may have to be discarded because of the subject's uneasiness or self-consciousness when confronted with a camera. After a short time, however, this uneasiness diminishes. Once that happens, a home video system can go a

long way to improve one's technique in almost any activity by using variable speeds, pauses, freeze-frames, and so forth. Over time it can also graphically demonstrate changes, either for better or for worse.

Business. A home video system can be a valuable asset to someone attempting to sell a product or a service that is not readily accessible or portable. It takes little imagination, for example, to see the enormous advantage to a real estate broker who uses videocassettes to show available property to prospective buyers. Several residential and commercial properties can be seen right in the broker's office, saving time, gas, and nerves. Video is a highly effective medium for sales presentations, demonstrations, and training sessions. Many large corporations have fairly sophisticated video facilities. But for smaller businesses a portable VCR and a small video camera can be highly useful selling tools.

Closed-circuit television (CCTV). While closed-circuit TV may require the services of a technician for proper installation, it should not be overlooked as an extremely valuable application of a home video system. CCTV is already being used as a security measure. It can also be used for babysitting and for keeping a watchful eye on someone in a sickroom.

Correspondence. If you have a friend or relative who lives some distance away and has a VCR that is compatible with yours, just imagine the infinite pleasures to be derived by exchanging "living" letters.

Last will and testament. Some people have actually resorted to having their last wills and testaments recorded on videotape. One attorney is reported as having said that "a lot of people are going to use it as a parting shot— to get to say things they've always wanted to say . . . Just think of the pleasure it would give a wealthy man to cut off his free-spending brother and then to explain it all in living color." (*Moneysworth,* December 1979) If you are similarly inclined, by all means have a good time. Just remember that, in general, wills must be in writing to be legal. A videotaped will should not be substituted for the

There are many commercial and industrial applications for a home video system, such as recording the progress of a building under construction. Exceptionally lightweight units like the one shown here are especially suited for such purposes. TECHNICOLOR, INC.

written document; rather, it should serve as a supplement to it.

The uses and pleasures of a home video system are limited only by its owner's imagination. We have suggested here only a few of those uses and pleasures.

Television has often been described—and denounced—as a passive medium. One simply sits and watches as the hips expand, conversation dissipates, the brain rots, and the imagination atrophies. There may be some validity to that viewpoint, although it is arguable (and I have, on more than one occasion, so argued). The fact remains that if television is a passive medium, video surely is not. By definition video directly involves the user. Even if you confine a home video system to viewing commercially available prerecorded cassettes and discs, you are actively involved in selecting and planning the kind of entertainment and instruction that comes into your own home.

With the addition of a camera, a basic home video system becomes a medium for entertainment, instruction, a personal family archive, and—dare we suggest it?—even creativity.

Epilogue: The Future

> . . . and we,
> Great in our hope, lay our best love and credence
> Upon thy promising fortune.
>
> —*All's Well That Ends Well*, III, iii

Kenneth Ingram, Senior Vice President of Sales and Marketing for the Magnavox Consumer Electronics Company, has predicted that "as video options become more popular, and creative minds begin to push the bounds of the medium, discs and cassettes will carve out their own style and programming realm—bringing new and exciting entertainment, educational, and instructional shows into the home of the eighties." Perhaps because of the specific interests of his company, Mr. Ingram failed to point out what must surely be obvious to even the most casual observer: Video will have an enormous impact on the sociological, economic, and artistic segments of our society.

Plain old commercial television has already opened fantastic vistas. There are no more hick towns and country bumpkins. Anyone who can afford a TV set has seen the world and has been an eyewitness to some of the most dramatic events in the history of the human race. We have been inside the halls of Congress and the halls of justice.

As I have tried to indicate throughout this book, the future of video—and nearly everything else—is at best uncertain. When one takes into account the various legal problems yet to be resolved, the technological obstacles to be overcome (including the incompatibility of several systems aimed at accomplishing the same end), rapidly advancing technologies, divergent philosophies, ethics, and morals—virtually any prediction that one would care to make, and virtually any esthetic declamation that one would care to utter, would be fair game for argument and contradiction.

Personally, I am prepared to make one statement which I believe can no longer be argued. As I stated at the conclusion of Chapter 10, the notion that video is a passive medium is simply no longer true. Not only does it have the capability of being a highly active medium but the degree of activism depends solely on the active participant. In the final analysis, what video can and cannot do is very much within your own control.

Armies of consultants and other experts have proclaimed that the TV screen will become the communications center of the home of the future. It will be a work station hooked up to a personal computer, so that fewer people will have to go into an office to do work. Already many managers and executives have computer terminals in their homes, making it possible to avoid crowds, public transportation, and drains on energy resources while they spend more time at home and perform their work. As that work becomes more computerized, and as the average TV set comes equipped with jacks, inputs, and outputs of various kinds as standard equipment, more and more people will be able to work at home, including those previously unable to work for money because of various constraints on their ability to travel.

It has also been predicted that *teletext* will soon be available in the United States on a wide scale. Essentially, teletext is an information bank. It makes available to the subscriber such things as TV listings, the latest news, weather information, travel information, and a host of other useful data that is obtained by connecting a specially equipped TV set to telephone lines. Versions of teletext are now available in Great Britain, France, Canada, and experimentally in the United States. There are some technological and philosophical difficulties that are hindering the development of teletext in this country, but it is probably only a question of time before it becomes widely available.

If predictions that the TV set will become a communications hub prove to be true, then we can expect to see a significant and dramatic change in the way we do business and in the business we do. It will be a simple matter to order food and other supplies from a supermarket—which will not be a supermarket at all, but a central distribution warehouse that arranges for home delivery of the order that has been placed through the TV-computer hookup. It will also be easy to pay for that order: A simple instruction relayed to a system that connects the computer, the TV screen, and telephone terminals can transfer funds from the purchaser's bank account to the supplier's.

As indicated earlier, motion picture exhibitors are greatly concerned over the probable change in entertainment habits. Those of us who are over forty have seen the flourishing of the great movie palaces, only to watch them sink into disuse and disrepair, ultimately to be converted into smaller, more intimate theaters. If, as predicted, video proliferates, we may see the re-emergence of the movie palace as a kind of vast entertainment center, specifically designed for people who want to go out occasionally for an evening or even a day.

It could happen. At this very moment there exists in a housing development in Scottsdale, Arizona, "The House of the Future," located near a planned community called Ahwatukie. The house's construction and operation involve several companies, including the developer who owns the property on which it is built, but it is primarily the baby of the Motorola Company's microprocessor division, which has equipped the house with five microcomputer systems that control indoor environment, outside security, and contain all kinds of data. These systems all operate through conventional TV sets that also receive conventional TV programs.

Who knows what else lies in store? Already engineers are working on three-dimensional television. Already the technology exists for interactive, two-way live television; before long you and I may be able to talk to each other through our video screens. Already people are predicting that the communications medium you are holding in your hands this very moment—the book—will be a thing of the past.

The demise of the book is being credited to the rise of the videodisc. It has to do with the videodisc's compactness and the random-access capability of the system. It is believed that just as books are now being used for a wide range of purposes, from entertainment and instruction to propaganda, videodiscs could similarly be used for the same purposes. Indeed, it is conceivable that videodiscs could be used much more effectively than books because, in addition to words, they can provide pictures that move and that show exactly what is being done or should be done.

A number of major magazines and book publishers are seriously contemplating entering the video field. Some videocassette "magazines" already exist. *Video Fashion Quarterly* bills itself as the world's first magazine on videotape. Each cassette offers a ninety-minute program showing the latest in women's fashions. Although *Video Fashion Quarterly* is intended primarily for commercial users—Revlon and Jordan Marsh are among its current subscribers—it gives the fashion news update far more effectively than any other medium could and offers an example of what can be accomplished by video magazines.

Instant Replay also claims to be the first magazine on videotape. (Perhaps they are both right: *Instant Replay* may be the first "publication" directed at the general viewer.) Each issue contains a dozen or so longer articles, columns, and features that run the gamut of subjects from air races to *The Rocky Horror Picture Show*. The cost is between $50 and $60 for a cassette that runs anywhere from a half hour to two hours.

I hope that the move toward the obsolescence of books can be slowed or even halted. There are, after all, certain aspects of books that are worth preserving. Esthetics, for example; practicality, for another. Furthermore, involvement with a book (except, perhaps, for one that is being read aloud) is highly personal and individual. It is possible to escape into or behind a book both physically and in-

tellectually. One can do so privately, even with other people in the room, a facility that no video system can ever offer. Nor can I conceive of a videodisc player, however small or portable they eventually become, being carried on a bus or subway, or being used to while away the time at the airport or in the bathroom. A book is a highly efficient and unique object. So far I have neither seen, nor can I conceive of, anything to replace its very special qualities.

Still, the future—as uncertain as it may be—is full of bright hope and promise. I vividly remember a feature story recently telecast on a local news show. The reporter was interviewing a woman who was celebrating her hundredth birthday. The reporter was holding an expensive microphone and the two were surrounded by highly sophisticated portable lights, hundreds of feet of cable, a TV camera, and complicated sound-recording equipment. Apparently oblivious to the thousands of dollars of technology around them, the reporter asked the hundred-year-old woman, "Have things changed much since you were a child?"

It was, of course, a stupid question. It would be a stupid question to ask even a ten-year-old. Over the past few decades technology has been plummeting onward at an almost frightening rate. Nowhere has this been more evident than in communications, and nowhere in communications has it been more evident than in home video.

It has been the purpose and hope of this book to open a few doors, not only to the technological but to the imaginative dimension of home video. It is a guide for beginners. We are standing together at the threshold of a future with enormous potential, one that goes beyond our wildest hopes and imaginings.

It would seem, therefore, that, after all, we are all just beginners.

Bibliography

Come, and take choice of all my library . . .

—*Titus Andronicus*, IV, i

Magazines

As one might expect in a burgeoning field, there are several burgeoning magazines dealing with home video. There are also several publications dealing with the commercial, industrial, and educational aspects of video. (More information about these can be obtained from your local librarian.) As a matter of fact, virtually every general consumer magazine has covered, at one time or another during recent months, some aspect of home video. It seems both understandable and natural that a number of photography magazines are also devoting considerable space to this field.

Listed below are publications devoted almost exclusively to home video. They are, in my opinion, ideally suited for beginners with little or no technical background. They are universally informative, generally cheerful, and manage to present their material in lay terms without sounding patronizing. They are listed here, more or less, in order of preference, although there is actually very little discernible difference among them.

Home Video, 475 Park Avenue South, New York, New York 10016

Video, 235 Park Avenue South, New York, New York 10003

Video Review, 325 East 75th Street, New York, New York 10021. At this writing *Video Review* is a relative newcomer to the field. I cannot, therefore, classify it along with the two preceding publications. It does seem to show promise, however, and is worth watching. Its main feature seems to be "250 reviews in every issue." These are capsule reviews of prerecorded material available on videocassettes.

Books

The books listed below are recommended for readers who are interested in going beyond the basic home video system. They are arranged here, more or less, in order of complexity, along with a few explanatory notes and comments.

Bensinger, Charles. *The Home Video Handbook,* 2nd edn. (1980: Video-Info Publications, P.O. Box 1507, Santa Barbara, California 93102). This handy little volume is an excellent introduction to the basics of equipment and production for those who require more technical details. If you want to do more than "plug it in and turn it on," this book will show you how.

Ogden, Andrew, and Steve Spence. *Jungle Video: A Practical Guide to Production* (1979: Jungle Video, Ltd., P.O. Box 148, Balboa Island, California 92662). The book's subtitle essentially describes its contents. This is a step-by-step guide to producing your own video programming with basic home video equipment.

Robinson, Richard. *The Video Primer* (1978: Quick Fox, 33 West 60th Street, New York, New York 10023). This book operates on the assumption that you are prepared to engage in serious video production. Many aspects of technology are explained; home video is covered in a three-page chapter.

Utz, Peter. *Video User's Handbook* (1980: Prentice-Hall, Englewood Cliffs, New Jersey 07632). This book also seems to assume that the reader is ready to go into video as an advanced hobbyist or even as a professional. A major advantage is that it covers a myriad of things that can go wrong and how to correct them.

Marsh, Ken. *Independent Video* (1974: Fireside/Simon & Schuster, 1230 Avenue of the Americas, New York, New York 10020). The best way to describe this book is to quote from its own jacket: "A complete guide to the physics, operation, and application of the new television for the student, the artist, and for community TV." There is a considerable amount of "heavy science" in this work. Everything is clearly illustrated by means of easy-to-read sketches and diagrams, so that the reader who cares enough will have a clear concept of exactly how things work.

Glossary

Good sentences, and well pronounced.

—The Merchant of Venice, I, ii

The glossary that follows is included here for two reasons. First, in your quest for video equipment and information, you are likely to come across terms that are unfamiliar to you. As long as you confine your interests to home video, chances are you will find those terms defined here. Second, it is highly recommended that you read through the glossary, from A to Z, two or three times to familiarize yourself with the words and phrases so common to home video.

In all fairness it should be pointed out that insofar as the entire field of video is concerned, this glossary is woefully incomplete. A great many terms which apply mostly to industrial, professional, and commercial television have been excluded. Several of the books described in the Bibliography have glossaries that include many of the more esoteric terms.

NOTE: Words in *italics* indicate cross-references to other parts of the Glossary.

AC: See *alternating current*.

AC/DC CONVERTER: A device that changes alternating current to direct current. (The latter is often required to operate video equipment.)

AFT: Automatic fine tuning (tuner).

AGC: See *automatic gain control*.

ALC: See *automatic level control* and *automatic light control*.

ALTERNATING CURRENT (AC): Standard American household electrical current of 120 volts. Also known as *line voltage*. Compare *direct current*.

APERTURE: The opening in a camera lens through which light passes. The size of the opening is designated in *f-stops*.

ASPECT RATIO: Refers to the size of the TV picture. This is always four units wide to every three units high. For television, therefore, the aspect ratio is 3:4 or 3 × 4.

ASSEMBLY EDITING: A method of editing in which various segments are copied from videotapes onto a single videotape in a desired sequence. (See Chapter 10.)

ATTENUATION: The reduction or turning down of a signal level.

AUDIO: Specifically, the sound portion of a TV program; more generally, any electronically produced sound.

AUDIO CUE: A sound that serves as a signal to indicate that something is about to happen. Used in TV productions as signals to prepare to shift cameras, microphones, and so forth.

AUDIO DUB: To change or add to the sound portion of the videotape by recording over, but without affecting, the video portion. Compare *dubbing.*

AUDIO HEAD: The unit on a videocassette recorder or other recording and/or playback device that receives the audio signal and registers it on the tape, or picks up that signal from the tape and plays it back.

AUDIO IN: The jack on a piece of equipment through which the audio signal is delivered.

AUDIO OUT: The jack on a particular piece of equipment through which an audio signal is fed out.

AUDIO TRACK: The portion of videotape on which the audio, or sound, is recorded.

AUTOMATIC GAIN CONTROL (AGC): An electronic circuit that automatically regulates an audio signal. See *gain.*

AUTOMATIC LEVEL CONTROL (ALC): Another term for automatic gain control.

AUTOMATIC LIGHT CONTROL (ALC): A circuit in a TV camera that automatically compensates for variations in levels of light.

AVAILABLE LIGHT: The lighting conditions normally in existence at the time a scene is to be taped or filmed and to which no supplementary lights have been added.

AZIMUTH: The angle at which the recording head in a videocassette recorder is placed.

BACKLIGHT: Light which comes from behind the subject (rather than from behind the camera), rendering an effect, that ranges from a rim or halo light on the subject to showing the subject in silhouette, the particular effect depending on the intensity of the light.

BACKSPACING: Rewinding the tape the equivalent of two or three frames to assure clean overlaps in editing.

BETA: One of two videocassette formats. Compare *VHS.*

BETASCAN: The system on Beta videocasette recorders that permits high- or variable-speed reverse and forward.

BIDIRECTIONAL MICROPHONE: One which picks up sound from two different directions. Compare *cardioid, directional, omnidirectional,* and *unidirectional microphone.*

B-LOAD: Designates a particular configuration for loading tapes in cassettes designed for use in Beta videocassette recorders.

BODY BRACE: A type of camera support that is carried over the upper portion of the body.

BOOM: A piece of equipment used to hold a light, microphone, or camera up and away from the recording camera's angle of view. Microphone and light booms are generally comprised of various arrangements of metal pipes. Camera booms are expensive and complicated pieces of machinery.

BURN: To damage or destroy a portion of the vidicon tube in a TV camera by focusing too long on a bright object, thereby permanently burning in the image on the tube. The result is a shadowy image of that object, no matter what the camera is being pointed at. Compare *image retention* and *lag.*

CAPSTAN: A small shaft in a videocassette recorder that is rotated by a motor and controls the speed at which the tape moves.

CARDIOID MICROPHONE: A type of directional microphone that picks up sound coming from the front and a little to the side, in a kind of heart-shaped pattern. Compare *omnidirectional,* and *unidirectional microphone.*

CASSETTE: A container, usually made of plastic, in which is enclosed video (or other recording) tape and certain mechanical features to allow the tape to operate with the appropriate equipment.

CATHODE-RAY TUBE (CRT): A vacuum tube that produces electron beams which are then transmitted to the face of the tube, where, depending on the tube's function, a phosphor coating is caused to glow or an oxide coating is activated to create voltage. The picture tube in a TV, the screen on a computer terminal, and the vidicon tube in a TV camera are all versions of CRTs.

CATV: Community antenna television; usually used to designate cable TV.

CCTV: See *closed-circuit television.*

CHANNEL: The frequency or band assigned to a television broadcast.

CHROMA, CHROMINANCE: The hue and saturation

of a video image (i.e., color quality and intensity).

CHROMA CONTROL: The control that adjusts for color.

CHROMIUM DIOXIDE: The magnetic material with which most videotapes are coated and on which the recordings, both audio and video, are made.

CLOSED-CIRCUIT TELEVISION (CCTV): Any self-contained television system such as is used for security, surveillance, conferences, and so forth; television that is not publicly broadcast.

CLOSE-UP (CU): A picture taken at close range. Compare *medium* and *long shot.*

C-MOUNT: The standard lens mount on most video cameras; a screw-in type mount.

COAXIAL CABLE, COAX: The type of cable generally used in most video systems because it is capable of carrying a broad range of frequencies with virtually no loss of signal.

COLOR STRIPE FILTER: A special filter mounted in front of a TV camera tube which enables the recording of color images.

COLOR TEMPERATURE: A means of measuring the amount of red or blue in a particular color for the purpose of optically or electronically making such adjustments as are necessary. Expressed in degrees Kelvin (°K).

COMPATIBILITY: The ability of one piece of equipment to be used in conjunction with another, or of *software* that can be used in units by various manufacturers.

CONDENSER MICROPHONE: A microphone that uses two condenser plates that convert sound waves to variations in voltage.

CONTROL TRACK: A track that runs along the full length of a videotape and carries electrical pulses that control the speed with which the tape travels.

CONTROL TRACK HEAD: The unit on a video tape recorder that responds to the electrical pulses on the control track.

CRT: See *cathode-ray tube.*

CUE: Any prearranged signal that indicates that some action or event is about to occur.

dB: See *decibel.*

DC: See *direct current.*

DECIBEL (dB): A unit used for measuring the volume of sound.

DEFINITION: The detail or sharpness of a TV image.

DEPTH OF FIELD: When a lens is focused on a subject, the area in front of the subject and behind the subject that is also in sharp focus is known as the depth of field or depth of focus. Depth of field varies with the size and quality of the lens and with the *f-stop* at which the lens is set.

DEW: A signal on a videocassette recorder indicating that there is too much humidity in the environment or in the machine itself and which automatically turns the unit off until drier conditions prevail.

DIAPHRAGM: The element in a microphone that vibrates when subjected to sound waves. The diaphragm vibrations are converted into variations in voltage, which in turn produce the sound or audio signal. The *iris* in a camera is also often called a diaphragm.

DIRECT CURRENT (DC): Electrical current that, unlike AC, maintains a constant, steady flow. Many electronic devices operate on direct current and require converters, usually built into the unit itself. Compare *alternating current.*

DIRECTIONAL MICROPHONE: A microphone that picks up sound only from the direction in which it is pointed. Compare *cardioid, omnidirectional,* and *unidirectional microphone.*

DROP-OUT: The loss of a portion of the TV picture; usually caused by worn or damaged videotape, with pieces of iron oxide missing, or by videotape heads that need cleaning.

DUBBING: Placing sound on the audio portion of a videotape. This may consist of background music, narration, atmospheric sound effects, or —for the adventuresome and fastidious— dialogue which must be synchronized with lip movements. Compare *audio dub.*

DYNAMIC MICROPHONE: A type of microphone that incorporates a coil of wire situated close to a magnet and which responds to the vibrations of the diaphragm, thus producing voltage.

ECU: Extreme closeup.

EDITING: The process of extracting scenes from various tapes or from disconnected portions of the same tape and rerecording them on another tape in a desired sequence. Compare *electronic editing.*

ELECTRET CONDENSER MICROPHONE: A highly sensitive microphone that operates on direct current, either through its own battery or the batteries in audio tape recorders and video cameras into which the microphone is built.

ELECTRON GUN: The cathode, heater, and bridge which together produce the electron beam in a *cathode-ray tube.*

ELECTRONIC EDITING: The term often used for the process described under *editing;* so named because, unlike film, no tape is actually cut and spliced.

ELECTRONIC VIEWFINDER: A miniature TV screen affixed to a video camera that allows the operator to view the scene the camera is picking up.

ERASE HEAD: The head on a video or audio recorder that erases or removes the signal already existing on the tape before recording new material.

FADE: To vary the strength of an audio or video signal for special effects, such as scene transitions. The term fade in means raising the signal from an extremely low level to one that is audible or visible; fade out means doing the reverse; fade to black means lowering the video signal until the screen goes black.

FOCAL LENGTH: The distance, measured in millimeters, between the optical center of a lens and the area or plane at which the image is to appear. (In film cameras the film is located in the image plane; in video cameras the vidicon tube is located in the image plane.) Focal length determines the horizontal angle of the lens's view. Lenses with long focal lengths bring the image in close; those with short focal lengths offer an extremely wide angle of view. See *telephoto, wide-angle,* and *zoom lens.*

FRAME: A complete television picture consisting of 525 horizontal lines.

FRAME FREQUENCY OR RATE: The speed with which single frames are shown. On television the frame frequency is usually thirty frames per second (fps).

F-STOP: The openings on a lens that control the amount of light passing through the lens are calibrated (i.e., measured) in f-stops. The higher the f-stop number, the smaller the opening and the less light that passes through. Compare *iris.*

GAIN: Signal amplification. Lowering the gain reduces the strength of the signal; raising the gain increases it. Applicable to both video and audio. See *automatic gain control.*

GENERATION: An original video or audio recording is said to be the first generation. A copy made from that becomes the second generation; a copy made from the second generation is known as the third generation, and so forth. In each successive generation the audio and video quality are diminished somewhat.

GLITCH: Anything that causes a distortion in the picture; also, inasmuch as this word has probably been adopted from the computer field, it can be used to describe any snag or difficulty of undetermined origin.

GUARDBAND: A band on a videotape that separates the video tracks from the audio and control tracks.

HARDWARE: Any piece of equipment that is essentially unalterable except through mechanical modification. Compare *software.*

HEAD: An electromagnetic component of a recording and/or playback system that either places electromagnetic pulses over the surface of recording tape as the tape passes it or retrieves the signals from the surface of the tape for playback.

HIGH DENSITY: Descriptive of videotape that contains an extremely high number of magnetic particles as compared to ordinary tapes.

IMAGE ENHANCER: Anything that improves the detail of an image. See *resolution.*

IMAGE RETENTION: The tendency of the vidicon tube in a television camera to hold onto the image for a short time even though the camera has been shifted to another scene or subject, producing a kind of smearing effect. This is also known as *lag.* When image retention becomes permanent, it is called *burn.*

INPUT SELECTOR: The control on VHS videocassette recorders used for selecting the appropriate recording input, such as the TV tuner, video camera, and so forth.

IPS: Inches per second; the standard unit of measurement to designate the speed with which tape travels through an audio or video recorder.

IRIS, IRIS DIAPHRAGM: A set of overlapping adjustable leaves that control the amount of light passing through a lens and into the camera. See *f-stop.*

JACK: A plug or connector; typically, one

through which some other component can be connected.

JOYSTICK: In video games, a lever used to control the image on the screen. The same term applies to a similar lever that positions a special effect on the screen.

KELVIN: See *color temperature*.

LAG: See *image retention*.

LENS SPEED: A designation indicating the ability of a lens to admit light. A fast lens has a wider maximum iris opening than a slow lens. See *f-stop* and *iris*.

LINE VOLTAGE: See *alternating current*.

LONG SHOT (LS): A picture taken from a considerable distance that covers a wide area. Compare *close-up* and *medium shot*.

MEDIUM SHOT (MS): A picture taken somewhere in the rather arbitrary range between a *long shot* and a *close-up*.

MIXER: An electronic device that blends sounds and/or pictures from various sources for presentation as a single entity.

M-LOAD: A designation for the method of loading the tape into a cassette that is used by VHS videocassette recorders.

MONITOR: A television set used for displaying the output of a video camera, video tape recorder, and so forth. Invariably it is incapable of receiving broadcast signals. Those that are are known as monitor/receivers.

NOISE: Any stray signal, in either audio or video, that interferes with the sound or picture. Compare *snow*.

NORMAL LENS: A lens which "sees," more or less, what a person would see if he or she were standing in the same position, allowing for a little falloff of peripheral vision. The term is an arbitrary one and can probably best be defined as a lens that is neither *telephoto* nor *wide angle* but somewhere in between.

OMNIDIRECTIONAL MICROPHONE: A microphone that picks up all of the sound surrounding it. Compare *bidirectional, cardioid, directional,* and *unidirectional microphone*.

OPEN REEL: See *reel-to-reel*.

OXIDE: The magnetic particles affixed to the surface of recording tape.

PANNING: Following action by standing in one position and swivelling the camera across a horizontal plane. Compare *trucking*.

PAUSE: The control on a videocassette recorder that temporarily halts the movement of the tape.

PHOTOFLOOD: An extremely bright light bulb ideal for amateur photography or videotaping.

PLAYBACK HEAD: See *head*.

PROGRAMMABLE VCR: A videocassette recorder that can be set in advance for automatic recording.

PROGRAM SELECTOR: The control on a videocassette recorder that determines what the VCR will transmit to the television screen.

PULSE: The variation of an electrical or magnetic signal over a specified period of time.

RADIO FREQUENCY (RF): The range of frequencies over which electrical waves are transmitted.

REEL-TO-REEL: Used to describe any recording unit that uses reels of tape that must be placed on, and removed from, the spindles, as opposed to a fully enclosed system, such as a cassette; also called *open reel*.

REGISTRATION: The proper overlapping of red, blue, and green signals in such a way as to provide an image of the proper color.

RESOLUTION: A somewhat arbitrary evaluation of the detail present in a video image.

RF: See *radio frequency*.

RF ADAPTOR: A unit which transforms video signals for transmission over radio frequencies.

ROLL: A problem with the vertical hold on a TV screen that causes the picture to appear to be rolling either up or down.

RPM: Revolutions per minute.

SCANNING: The movement of an electron beam over a TV tube.

SEARCH: A videocassette capability which permits the location of some particular point on the tape.

SNOW: A form of *noise*.

SOFTWARE: In general, anything that contains a program. Videocassettes and videodiscs qualify as software. Compare *hardware*.

SPEED SWITCH: The control on a VCR that sets the speed at which the VCR is to operate.

SPLICING: The cutting and rejoining of sections of tape.

STORYBOARD: A sheet of paper on which blank TV screens have been drawn or printed; used to plan out shooting or editing sequences.

SYNC: Video jargon for synchronize, synchronization, or synchronizers. In general, sync refers to the pulses that maintain sychronization between the horizontal and vertical picture signals.

SYNC GENERATOR: The circuit that provides the sync signals required to coordinate various components of the video system with respect to the video signal and to each other.

TAPE PATH: The path along which the tape travels on its journey past the various heads and around *capstans* and rollers.

TEARING: An effect created in a video image when the horizontal sync is malfunctioning. Compare *sync.*

TELE-CINE: Any process that converts program material on film to a video medium.

TELEPHOTO LENS: A lens with a long focal length, permitting close-ups even though the camera is relatively far from the subject.

TRACK: The section running along the tape on which audio or video material has been recorded.

TRUCKING: Following action by moving the camera along a horizontal plane, such as by walking or on a dolly. Compare *panning.*

UNIDIRECTIONAL MICROPHONE: A microphone that picks up sound only from the direction in which it is pointed. Compare *bidirectional, cardioid, directional,* and *omnidirectional microphone.*

VARIABLE FOCAL LENGTH LENS: See *zoom lens.*

VCR: See *videocassette recorder.*

VHS: Video Home System; a VCR format. Compare *Beta.*

VIDEOCASSETTE: A closed plastic container with one reel of videotape and one empty, or take-up reel.

VIDEOCASSETTE RECORDER (VCR): A device which records and plays back program material using videocassettes. VCRs also perform other functions, all of which are described in detail in Chapter 4.

VIDEODISC: A disc closely resembling a phonograph record which contains video programs. See Chapter 5.

VIDEO IN: A jack on a video component into which a video signal is transmitted.

VIDEO OUT: A jack on a component from which a video signal is transmitted.

VIDEO TAPE RECORDER (VTR): Any of various devices, ranging from those used in the home to highly sophisticated equipment used in commercial studios, that record video and audio material on magnetic tape. A videocassette recorder is a VTR.

VIDICON TUBE: The tube in video cameras that transforms light into electrical signals.

VIGNETTING: A condition in which the central image is surrounded by a dark frame. This can result from a lens hood that is too long or because a camera, for some reason, cannot cover an area equivalent to that shown on the screen.

VOICE-OVER: A narration of a film or tape, usually dubbed in after the shooting. Compare *dubbing.*

VU METER: Volume unit meter; an indicator that shows the level of volume being recorded.

WHITE BALANCE: The adjustment in a video camera, frequently automatic, that produces well-balanced white, thereby establishing the relative brightness of other objects in the scene.

WIDE-ANGLE LENS: A lens that encompasses an extremely wide area. See *focal length.* Compare *telephoto* and *zoom lens.*

WINDSCREEN: A kind of glove or sleeve, usually made of a substance similar to foam rubber material, that is placed over a microphone to minimize the noise generated by wind blowing past the microphone when recording outdoors.

ZOOMING: Operating the zoom lens while filming or recording for special effects. Zooming in creates the effect of moving in close to the subject; zooming out creates the effect of backing away from the subject.

ZOOM LENS: A lens whose focal length is variable. Depending upon its overall length, a zoom lens can go from wide-angle to telephoto without the camera being moved. See *focal length, telephoto lens,* and *wide-angle lens.*